Risk Assessment Framework

Risk Assessment Framework
Successfully Navigating Uncertainty

Ray W. Frohnhoefer, MBA, PMP, CCP

Risk Assessment Framework: Successfully Navigating Uncertainty

ISBN-13: 978-0-9893770-7-2 (paperback)
ISBN-13: 978-0-9893770-8-9 (e-book)

Cover design by Luisito C. Pangilinan
Copyediting aided by Microsoft Word, Grammarly, and Hemingway Editor
References supported by Zotero
Indexing supported by DEXter by the Editorium

This second edition combines *The Risk Assessment Framework* and *The Risk Assessment Framework Implementation Guide*, initially published in 2014. For information about copyright, permissions, bulk discounts, or purchase, contact:

PPC Group, LLC
3450 3rd Avenue
Suite 309
San Diego, CA 92103
USA
https://ppcgroup.us
https://accidentalpm.online
http://rayfrohnhoefer.com

"Every project has risk, so every project manager should know how to deal with it! Risk identification, mitigation, and management are difficult concepts for new (and sometimes even experienced) project managers. In his book *Risk Assessment Framework,* Ray provides an easy-to-follow framework. Ray also provides the tools necessary to make the project manager successful. It's a 'must have' book for both education and future reference."

"Ray reveals the power of identifying 'risk events that can have positive outcomes' for organizational initiatives in his new book. *Risk Assessment Framework: Successfully Navigating Uncertainty* delivers a practical approach for project, program, and portfolio managers to unlock the secrets of risk and expose the opportunity. I highly recommend this as a guidebook for project leaders working on projects of varying size and complexity for any size initiative in their organization."

"Ray's done a fantastic and thorough job of addressing the topic of risk management. You'll find the tools outlined in the book to be very helpful in reducing the uncertainty associated with project risk."

"Thanks for giving me an opportunity to read this book. You have done an excellent job with this book.

It is a comprehensive book on risk assessment and mitigation within a simple and easy-to-understand framework. The framework has been supported with subsequent detailed descriptions of various components of the framework.

The tools and templates you have provided will be a great help to anyone doing the risk assessment. This is an excellent reference book on this subject for anyone managing projects, which is a key for successfully completing the project.

I am glad I read this book. Also, I recommend anyone in the project management field to read this book and keep it for easy reference. It is worthwhile and will add value to your endeavor in risk assessment."

— Sumith Kahanda, Ph.D., M.Sc., P.Eng., PMP, CSSGB
Project Manager, SaskWater
Saskatoon, Canada

"As someone who has been in the project management world my entire career, Ray has done a great job of capturing the importance of Risk Management in the process of executing an effort. With every industry and organization, there will be subtle shifts in the pieces used, but Ray has captured the core elements (like a recipe) that you will need to succeed and minimize the overall risk for any effort."

— Lorelie M Kaid, PMP, MBA, CCMP, CSP, CSPO
VP, Enterprise Project Management, WSECU

"Ray Frohnhoefer is part of the international bedrock of project management. With this book's focus on risk management, he helps young project managers bring predictability and order into their projects and prepare for situations when this is not possible.

Seasoned project managers will benefit from a streamlined framework that helps navigate an often-confusing set of tasks, whose mastership can make the difference between success and failure of a project."

— Oliver F. Lehmann, MSc, PMP
Project Management Trainer, Author, and Speaker
Munich, Germany

"Most professionals have seen or can name many spectacular and costly failures, which arose because the risks were not addressed systematically. Having observed countless projects and initiatives globally, my hunch is that it is difficult to communicate because risk assessment and implementation seem to be theoretical. This results in not getting enough resources and capacity to maximize the opportunities and minimize the threats.

Ray's welcome update of his earlier works on Risk Assessment gives you a structure to get over the hurdles and address risks head-on. Whether you are a risk expert or not, this is a book you should not miss."

— Dr Deasún Ó Conchúir CEng FIET FIEI PMP
Project Consultant, Scatterwork
Switzerland

"A practical book loaded with tested and tried risk management strategies by an experienced author. A must-have desk reference manual for every project and risk manager."

— **Harjit Singh, MS, MBA, PMP, CSM, LSSBB, ITILv4**
Sigma PM Consulting, Inc.
Sacramento, California

"This practical and 360° approach risk management book, complete with the list of questions to ask, points to implement, to review, and to monitor, will help you in creating your organization's roadmap for risk management. I highly recommend the *Risk Assessment Framework* by Ray W. Frohnhoefer to leaders of every organization, especially those implementing digital transformation."

— **Marie Nadia Vincent, MBA, PMP**
Digital Transformation Executive Advisor
IT Management Consultant
Author, *Leveraging Digital Transformation*

"I believe this is a must-read edition for all those who want to explore and assess 'known unknowns' and unknowable uncertainties. This book demonstrates the application of best risk assessment practices."

— **Kashif Zafeer, MCA, PMP**
Project Management Consultant
New Delhi, India

About the Author

Ray Frohnhoefer is the Managing Partner of PPC Group, LLC, helping aspiring, new, and accidental project managers and their organizations improve project management practice. Products and services include international bestsellers in Business Project Management, education, corporate training, and consulting.

Ray has led consulting teams in many industries and locations over his 40-year career. Notable projects include:

- rolling out a UNIX development environment to 400+ developers in 16 locations
- testing electronic voting equipment with a team of 30 for San Diego County
- patenting an estimating tool used by a global Project Management Office.

No stranger to virtual, global teams, he has been working with them his entire career.

Ray has had a dual career in project management and training. For eight years, he was an author, editor, and lecturer for the Edison Engineering Advanced Course in Computers. He has been teaching project management and business analysis classes for UC San Diego Extension for 18 years.

A long-time Project Management Institute (PMI) volunteer, Ray served as President of the PMI San Diego Chapter in 2005.   In 2006 he was the first official PMI Region Mentor for Southwest North America.   He has supported several international PMI committees and groups over the past 15 years. Ray also helped the PMI

Educational Foundation create its first professional development scholarship, and he continues to support their work.

Ray holds an undergraduate degree in Mathematics with a Computer Science concentration and an MBA degree in Technology Management. He is a PMI Leadership Institute Masters Class graduate and a Certified Computer Professional (CCP).

Dedication

To my loving husband: Thank you for being here to encourage and support my work. Love you always!

—Ray W. Frohnhoefer

Table of Contents

List of Figures, Tables, and Equations

Preface

Long before the publication of *A Guide to the Project Management Body of Knowledge* (PMBOK® Guide) as a standard, my work shaped my thoughts on navigating uncertainty. An early project where I played a leading technical role failed due to multiple risks. I identified many, but none had appropriate responses. I never understood why management ignored them. In the end, an improbable and impactful event dealt a final blow to both the project and the company. As a result, a competitor closed 45 of 50 potential sales of the product under development. In Mountain View, California, the Computer History Museum memorialized our project as a footnote to the successful project display (it says "we also tried").

In the early 1980s, when I formally began my first official project management role, I decided to take a different approach. Knowing many things can set back a project, I asked the team to look for opportunities to complete the project faster and with higher quality. Our project scope was to develop three significant pieces of software to dramatically increase the productivity of 50 software engineers (reduce up to 24 hours of work to somewhere under an hour). We found that other organizations completed similar projects in 5-6 years with 8-12 resource teams. We had nowhere near that level of resources, and management expected results in a year or so.

A few of the identified and acted upon opportunities included:

- For one piece of software, we used an existing user's guide rather than spending the time to write a new specification.

- For component, we identified existing software done by another team, which just needed modification of around 20-30% of the code.
- We completed the designs of shared files and routines for the three software systems first, so there would be little changes later impacting work progress.
- We conducted early trials with a willing subset of the engineers to help promote the effort and ease the others' conversion.

Also, we did look at threats. We found a political threat – we were planning to develop the system using a higher-level language. We knew many "old school" engineers would object, telling us it would not be sufficiently efficient. To avoid the problem, we developed a few of the critical algorithms early. We compared them to the existing system to show that they were superior. When the inevitable objections arose, we pulled out our data and gave a demonstration – the issue never came up again.

Four resources and one summer intern completed the project, and in just over one year, all 50 engineers were using it. After finding and fixing fewer than a half dozen bugs, the software operated and ran continuously for more than ten years.

After these early brushes with navigating uncertainty, I continued to exercise common sense throughout my career. I made it a point to see if there were possible improvements to the project, knowing this would protect us in the event of unidentified issues. Fast forward to 2001, and I was working as a project management methodologist for the global Project Management Office (PMO) of a major software company. The PMBOK® Guide – 2000 Edition had a newly developed chapter on risk management. Once I read it, how I wished this had been available all those years before.

During my tenure with the PMO, I began to craft a new service, a risk assessment workshop, which would be mandatory for projects worth $50M and above. It included a framework compliant, yet different in some key respects, with the PMBOK® Guide. Some trials of the new service conducted by the field project managers showed tremendous success. But before project completion, the company failed due to issues of its own making.

Over the next ten years or so, whenever I could, I worked on the material and used it in my practice of project management. I continued to research the topic and began to integrate it into my classes. I added a variety of tools and templates and continuously improved the documentation. I envisioned having a simpler and more scalable framework than what the PMBOK® Guide offered. The framework focused more on "how" rather than on "what." I envisioned risk management practiced in a non-prescriptive, flexible, and scalable manner. A provided framework and an implementation guide would help project managers better integrate risk management into project management practice. In 2014, I published my work in two volumes: *The Risk Assessment Framework* and *The Risk Assessment Framework Implementation Guide*.

Between 2015 and 2017, I made some modest annual updates, correcting errors and keeping up with new developments. I was happy with the work, which at the time, contained valuable implementation information. But with the late 2017 publication of the PMBOK® Guide – Sixth Edition, I knew more work would be needed. There were still parts of the framework and its implementation that were not fully documented. By mid-2018, I started thinking about the second edition, the book you are reading now.

This book combines *The Risk Assessment Framework* and *The Risk Assessment Framework Implementation Guide* as a newly updated and expanded second edition. Section I, The Risk Assessment Framework, details a flexible, scalable framework that applies to all initiatives of any type.

Section II, Achieving Success with the Risk Assessment Framework, reveals how to create a supportive environment, tailor the framework, identify and document critical decisions, and build supporting tools and techniques to ensure a successful implementation. The focus is on a risk management plan, a robust risk log to hold all risk information and data, and a risk assessment workshop (RAW) to address the risk assessment framework's critical steps with the stakeholders.

Section III, Tools and Techniques Supporting the Risk Assessment Framework, includes those tools and templates necessary to support the risk assessment workshop and the other risk management processes. One notable addition is the Risk Response Planning Process.

There are two new and unique features of this book:

1. The word "project" does not appear outside of examples. Research, practice, experience, and feedback show that the framework applies to all initiatives, whether a project, program, portfolio management, operations, or other initiatives.
2. Opportunities are emphasized over threats. Too many organizations fail to implement robust risk management because they "do not want to discuss negative things." If that is the case, they can make risk management about positive opportunities only and accrue benefits that offset some of their unidentified threats.

For aspiring, new, or accidental project managers or managers of other initiatives, consider learning and applying the basic framework with minimal tailoring. Focus on constructing a risk management plan, holding a risk assessment workshop using only brainstorming, and learning how to apply one of the two supplied risk log templates. Intermediate managers in an environment without a reliable risk management process should tailor the framework to meet specific initiative and organizational needs. If the environment has a risk management process, do a gap analysis between the methods presented in this book and current practices. And more advanced managers should also consider a gap analysis and adopt a mindset of continuous improvement.

Access to downloadable and editable forms and templates to guide implementation work is provided with this book. Here is what is new and different in the second edition:

- Both previous volumes combined into one book of three major sections
- The added emphasis that the framework applies to all forms of initiatives, from projects, programs, portfolios, and manufacturing to business operations
- Addition of critical success factors for each framework step
- Opportunities emphasized by addressing them ahead of threats
- Improved implementation content, including creating an environment supportive of success, a model risk management plan, added details for risk assessment workshops, and considerations for developing a supportive and functional RAID log
- Expanded coverage of tools and techniques
- Expanded materials and explanations throughout
- Improvements to all the downloadable materials

- Availability of an instructor site for trainers and educators who want to use the book and materials

Acknowledgments

There were so many people involved with this book that the best way to start is, "I'm sorry if I have left out your name."

First, I would like to thank Dr. John Estrella. John is an incredible business coach and mentor – all of us who work with him have experienced extraordinary transformations for our businesses. Without John's guidance, this book would probably still be an idea.

Next, I'd like to thank the many global professionals who have helped by reading, editing, and giving feedback and guidance for this book: Charles Adams (USA), Adel Al-Moghadawi (Saudi Arabia), Upendra Babu (India), Greta Blash (USA), Naomi Caietti (USA), Murray Grooms (Canada), Ayodeji Ishmael (Nigeria), Bob Jewell (USA), Sumith Kahanda (Canada), Lori Kaid (USA), Sandeep Khanna (USA), Pramit Kumar (India), Nitin Kundeshwar (USA), Oliver Lehmann (Germany), Corinna Martinez (USA), Deasún Ó Conchúir (Switzerland), Harjit Singh (USA), Jennifer Tharp (USA), M. Nadia Vincent (Belgium), and Kashif Zafeer (India). Your inputs and insights have been invaluable.

I would also like to thank the staff at California Southern University and UC San Diego Extension for their encouragement and support of this project. Also, my students in courses who have used the previous edition and updates. The feedback provided is always invaluable in shaping updates to course materials and books.

And finally, I would like to thank the many folks who follow me on social media: Facebook (including group PM360 and page Project Management), LinkedIn, and Twitter. Your encouragement has been invaluable in motivating the writing of this book.

#NAVIGATINGUNCERTAINTY

Introduction

What is a Framework?

A framework is a simple, basic conceptual structure of a process, adaptable to fit the needs and circumstances of initiatives (e.g., projects, programs, operations, even collections of activities). Robust frameworks (known as *shikumi* in Japanese) allow a company to change and weather changes quickly. A useful framework is usable by a small initiative and usable across the organization and organizations (Mikitani 2019).

Hiroshi "Mickey" Mikitani, the CEO of Rakuten, Inc., used frameworks to quickly assemble the forty companies and services in the business portfolio (Mikitani 2013). For example, with an extensive Internet service portfolio, Rakuten acquired one infrastructure monitoring application and made modifications as necessary to fit the specific business or service.

According to Wikipedia's "Business Model" entry (Wikipedia 2021), "Technology-centric communities have defined 'frameworks' for business modeling." Frameworks can quickly fill gaps where no process exists or guide the improvement of existing methods. They integrate well with business strategy and can improve operations.

The idea of a framework is not industry-specific. Frameworks can align strategy, products, and operations in virtually any industry, organization, or other environments.

About this Framework

This book provides a complete framework and a recommended means of implementation to establish a comprehensive, reusable, and sustainable risk management methodology for any initiative (e.g., projects, programs, operations). Tools, templates, forms, and guidance provide support for the implementation of the framework. It is up to the initiative manager to review the framework, tailor the framework to be appropriate for the initiative as needed, and choose tools and techniques to support the tailored framework.

This framework started nearly 20 years ago as a necessary process for complex software projects of $50M+ in value and typically lasting for one to five years. Risk assessment workshops, the recommended implementation of the framework were a requirement to improve project success. Although originating in the software industry, the framework includes best practices applicable to any industry or initiative. For example, implementing a good risk management plan is a crucial step in reducing construction claims, assuring quality manufacturing, and achieving business success. Users of the framework have applied it to other types of initiatives, such as programs and operations (e.g., manufacturing).

Research has shown the value of a concrete approach to risk management. In March 2013, the Project Management Institute's Pulse of the Profession report revealed that less than two-thirds of projects meet their actual business goals and 17 percent fail outright. Financially, this equates to 13.5 cents of every project dollar being unrecoverable. On the other hand, high-performing organizations that adopt project-management best practices have a critical advantage and see their success rates go up to over 90 percent (PMI 2013).

Further research in 2015 showed that risk management practice plays a significant role in meeting primary project goals. For those organizations applying a formal risk management approach, 73% of projects met their objectives, 61% finish on time, and 64% are within the approved budget (PMI 2015).

Risk management transcends projects, however. The ISO 31000:2018 standard "places more emphasis on both the involvement of senior management and the integration of risk management into the organization" (ISO 2018). Risk occurs in all initiatives at all levels of any enterprise.

Risk management is an often-overlooked or incorrectly utilized process, contributing significantly to failures (Standish 1995; Yazdanifard and Ratsiepe 2011; Scheid 2009; Lim 2019; PMI 2015). Good risk management does not just work with the obvious and immediately known risks; it digs deeper and assists in revealing previously unidentified risks. It looks for positives and negatives. In the process, it prepares the initiative to handle better the unknown risks likely to arise.

An essential aspect of risk management is that risk events can have positive outcomes, such as increased revenues, shortened schedules, or more effective resource utilization. These "positive risks" are known as "opportunities" and are managed in the same manner as any risk (PMI 2017). In addition to increasing the positive impacts on initiatives, added benefits of following a robust and appropriately scaled risk management process include:

- Improving the ability to anticipate changes and increase organizational agility
- Improving the ability of initiatives to deliver strategy
- Reducing the expense of preventive actions and the need for reactive measures
- Generating awareness of uncertainty while improving the predictability of outcomes
- Improving decision-making and resilience when unidentified events do occur

Risks with positive and negative outcomes are often interrelated. For example, there may be an opportunity to leverage a current product to create a new product as a unique revenue opportunity. Still, the additional work might burn out the project team. Carefully define "how" and "when" to accomplish the goal and leverage the opportunity without creating new threats.

At a minimum, risk management should occur within the lowest level initiatives (usually projects) in an organization. It seamlessly integrates with project management and is not only for a time of crisis. Risk management must be proactive and used with all projects to communicate an awareness of risk to all stakeholders. It is an ongoing process to subject to periodic review and revision.

Our experience indicates risk management does not require high overhead. Most small-to-medium enterprises and up to moderately complex initiatives can complete a risk assessment workshop (RAW) in under two days. An average initiative team can complete the entire process in a week or less. Larger, more complex initiatives may require up to a month (duration, not effort) to successfully collect and analyze the necessary data. Saving the project-to-project and initiative-to-initiative results may also reduce time if future projects or initiatives share similar risks.

Finally, this framework is not specific to business – it can play a role in your management of personal risks as well. Examples include:

- When considering a significant personal investment or investment decision (e.g., will my invested funds be safe? Will I get the best return on my investment?)
- When planning to build or remodel a home (e.g., how do I assure workers' safety? What happens if a deadline is not met? What quality of materials will be used?)
- When you are in a volunteer role leading initiatives (e.g., leading a fundraising campaign, managing a project to build a home, planning a major event)
- When planning personal travel (e.g., what will the weather be? What do I need to do for my safety? How can I get the lowest cost for my trip?)

Do not Treat Risk Like a Four-Letter Word

Some organizations do not support a culture that allows for the discussion of "bad things." Without the freedom to discuss problems and solutions, negative events are "swept under the carpet." One company I worked with had a weekly Monday "all department heads" meeting. It was mostly an hour and a half of everyone patting themselves on the back.

One week, I suggested that I had a problem that would benefit from the other department heads' inputs while we were all together. I was cut off and told we did not discuss the negatives and that I had to bring a solution. Of course, this was a "catch-22" because (a) we could not discuss it in the meeting, (b) most other department heads did not want to have discussions about issues one-on-one either, and (c) the discussion would be much more effective with all the right people together. What a way to set up an organization for failure!

Another frequent reason risk is not discussed is that it takes too long, has no benefit, etc. Yet clearly, there are lost opportunities and unwanted consequences of some of the actions. On an early software project I managed, I made sure we spent approximately 25% of planning time. I had the opportunity to hire the team, so I looked for people that wanted to be engaged in the project. We looked at many aspects of the project during planning, including anticipating political hurdles, correctly ordering the tasks for maximum efficiency, and looking for reusable code opportunities. And when we had an option, I brought promising interns into the group to help.

Overall, we finished the project in about a year, with four resources and an occasional intern. Later, I found out that similar projects in other companies were taking 10-12 resources up to 5 years to complete. Also, post-project, fewer than a dozen bugs were discovered, and one new feature was added. After that, the software was executed more than one million times over ten years and was still used when I left the company. Do you still think planning and managing is a waste of time?

Do not allow excessive "positivity" to keep you from doing what is necessary. One of the first things we need to do is work with project sponsors and senior management to change the culture. Positive thinking is so popular, yet expert psychologists agree that there is a need for more realism.

Genuinely successful leaders should love bad news. When they hear bad news, they need to make a conscious effort to see the positives and the potential for lessons learned. They must create an environment where bad news is welcome, challenging themselves and their teams to rise to the occasion and solve problems (Marr 2014).

New York University researched 800 people dieting. Half were given realistic assessments. When this group failed to lose weight, researchers challenged them to consider how they would meet their next goal – no excuses. The other half were told, "great job, good going," regardless of the outcome. Which group do you think was more successful in meeting their goals? The group with the realistic assessments, of course.

Hearing positive feedback led to complacency – "I'm doing great so I can have that bigger portion." What researchers found is that we need to perform what they call "mental contrasting." This is how we can meet our goals. We need to think: "if this happens, then I will do that......." (Johannessen 2012).

We are going to take another look at culture and calculated risks later in the presentation. But these are perfectly acceptable. However, to do this properly, you need to identify the probability and impacts of the risks correctly. You cannot just "bet the ranch." I worked for a company where the founder "bet the ranch" – the entire company was debt-funded in anticipation of a single product's development and sale. The founder's ability to get additional funding eventually ran out before the product was completed and any sales were made.

Also, do not be afraid to speak to and "sell" the opportunity side. Organizations of positive thinkers will appreciate that part more. There are positive components to risk, which we will look at shortly. This text always puts opportunities first, ahead of threats.

We need to spread how easy this can be and the potential rewards for using the framework.

An initial implementation of the framework is possible in hours, not days or weeks. Showing executives how easy it can be will help to get them on board with changing the culture. I have found that by using the framework, large complex initiatives can complete a robust risk assessment in about a week, and most average initiatives can complete one in under a day.

SECTION I: THE RISK ASSESSMENT FRAMEWORK

"Life is inherently risky. There is only one big risk you should avoid at all costs, and that is the risk of doing nothing."

– Denis Waitley

CHAPTER 1

DEFINITIONS AND OVERVIEW

Basic Definitions

Before diving into the framework, some standard definitions need to be understood. Overall, risk management is primarily about managing and navigating uncertainty. "Risks" are uncertainties that may cause initiatives to deviate from their defined initial plans. Risk has two major components

1. uncertainty, probability, likelihood, or chance
2. impact, consequences, or costs (PMI, 2017)

A risk with a favorable or positive impact is known as an "opportunity." Carefully managed opportunities can benefit both initiatives and the organizations executing them. For example, research might identify reusable code for a software project. Not understanding the code may present an element of risk; however, devoting time to analysis may result in time savings by having some work completed early. If the project ends sooner, the organization has an opportunity to begin another potentially critical project more shortly.

Additional examples of opportunities may include:

- Deciding to add sponsorship opportunities to an event may increase the budget
- Building a home on a pre-existing foundation may save time and cost
- Using sustainable energy instead of fossil fuel may earn a tax credit
- A small island nation may promote eco-tourism to add to the local economy
- Unexpectedly, a significant piece of equipment may still function well beyond its useful life if it was a carefully considered purchase
- By using different materials at no extra cost, the life of a bridge may be extended from 100 to 1,000 years

A risk with unfavorable or negative impact is known as a "threat" (be aware that many without a robust risk management background may refer to these as risks). Examples of threats include:

- Work stoppages caused by accidents or inclement weather
- A sole-source supplier may sell their business to your competition
- A backhoe may break down and need expensive repairs
- A small, expensive electronic component may be a target for theft
- A new product malfunction may necessitate a recalled
- Land needed for a right-of-way may not be easily acquired

The framework addresses both opportunities and threats. One typically expects only threats when discussing risks; however, this is a part of the long-standing definition in PMI's *A Guide to the Project Management Body of Knowledge*. Unfortunately, many practitioners still focus on threats rather than treating opportunities with equal (and possibly even more significant) importance.

Opportunities are often confused with benefits. The difference between the two is timing – opportunities have not yet occurred. They become benefits when a risk trigger (an event, condition, or other sign signaling that the risk is imminent) has occurred to make the opportunity actionable. Similarly, threats are often confused with issues. Threats are events that have not yet happened. They become issues when a risk trigger causes the event to happen. Examples of risk triggers for opportunities and threats include:

- Searching for reusable code for a project is an opportunity – once found and utilized, the reusable code is a benefit
- Bad weather is a threat to a construction project - the day a tornado is forecast, bad weather becomes an issue
- A new product malfunctions – when a recall is needed, it becomes an issue
- Installing solar panels earns a tax credit

Sometimes risk triggers can be encouraged (for opportunities) or prevented (for threats) before they occur. Sometimes it may be necessary to deal with the positive or negative consequences when the risk trigger happens. From a practical viewpoint, addressing issues is often referred to as "fire fighting," while actions to prevent the risk trigger can be considered "fire prevention."

One possible aid to dealing with risks is to review a list of universal risks. These are risks that may apply to any project, regardless of project type or industry. Budget and schedule overruns are just two of many possible universal risks. The International Council on Systems Engineering (INCOSE) and the Project Management Institute's Risk Specific Interest Group (PMI Risk-SIG) studied the issue of universal risks in 2002. They published a list of approximately 400 of them (Hall and Hulett 2002). Some examples of common project risks include:

- Scope creep
- Technical or design disagreements/conflict
- Lack of executive sponsorship
- Missed requirements
- Poorly managed requirements

While this report and list are not readily available, one strategy to follow would be to develop your list of universal risks appropriate to your organization and initiatives. Saving risk logs over time will allow you to effectively identify common risks to all initiatives and move them into an accessible list.

Sources of Risks

Risks impacting initiatives can come from many different sources, making it challenging to think through all the possibilities. Suppose a project team is working on a new drug and following the US Food and Drug Administration (FDA) rules. While FDA oversight protects future drug recipients, the FDA regulations are not adequate to shield a project from business and other initiative risks.

As a further aid to understanding and discussing risk, create a short list of risks for use as a prompt. Having a means of categorization can be useful in thinking through all the possibilities. Also, by putting all risks into categories where each category has common attributes, it is possible to develop strategies for handling more than one risk at a time. For this framework, consider the following categories:

- Client-Driven: Initiative clients, sponsors, and others from the client organization typically create client-driven opportunities and threats by their actions. Example opportunities and threats in this category include the following when driven by clients:

- o Scope change
- o Contractual changes
- o Schedule changes
- o Changed measures of performance

- Internal: These opportunities and threats are often related to the initiative selection or governance processes (e.g., project or program management methodology, in-house manufacturing operations). For example:
  - o Moving initiatives forward without a charter
  - o Multiple projects within a program sharing the same, limited resources
  - o Multiple projects in a portfolio sharing the same, limited resources
  - o Budget constraints caused by other initiatives with overruns

- External: These are opportunities and threats outside of the initiative and the organization(s) conducting or receiving the outcome(s) or output(s) of the initiative. Examples include the following:
  - o Social, political, and economic conditions such as inflation or wars
  - o Environmental impacts (e.g., a species will become extinct as the result of a project)
  - o Technology changes (e.g., the batteries planned for use by the program are now obsolete)

- Initiative Life Cycle: Within the initiative life cycle itself, opportunities and threats emerge as the initiative) moves from phase-to-phase. Include a review of all initiative planning documents, preferably line-by-line, to uncover these risks. Examples of these opportunities and threats revolve around situations such as the following:
  - o Questions of authority and responsibility

- o Initiative charter (e.g., a weak charter means a limited understanding of the actual scope required)
- o Decision making (e.g., following a good decision-making process leads to more effective decisions)
- o Strength of planning
- o Requirements management (e.g., requirements are not traceable, leading to unanswered requirements questions)
- o Budgets and Schedules
- o Contracts
- Regulatory: Regulatory opportunities and threats are risks generated by changes to laws, rules, and regulations that might occur based on governmental or organizational policy changes. While this category is essential to all initiatives, it is crucial to initiatives within highly regulated industries or controlled environments. For example:
  - o Licensing and regulatory changes
  - o Changes to FDA labeling requirements
  - o Sales tax law changes impacting resource pricing
  - o Project Management Office changes policy for project governance

Figure 1 illustrates how the categories relate to projects. The chart shows potential high-level risks of initiatives and their categories to consider when identifying risks. Since good examples generally relate to the type of initiative, a project is used as the initiative type (see Project Life Cycle in the illustration). Modify this illustration for other forms of initiatives, which need their unique life cycles substituted (e.g., program life cycle).

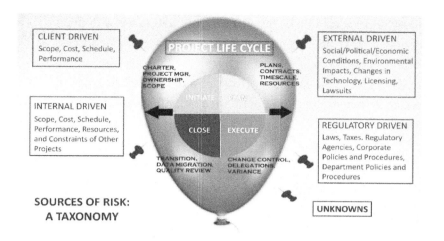

Figure 1. Sources of Risk: A Taxonomy

Most large, complex projects have significant elements of risk. They may range from the threat of failure in delivery, risk of cost and time overruns, or threat of external circumstances reducing the delivery of benefits. To be fully effective, initiative managers must seek to create an environment where the tangible deliverables can realize their full use and manage the risk within the life cycle. Such an environment may require the inclusion of some reasonable controls such as:

- An initiative charter or similar document (e.g., contract, statement of work) providing expectations and an initial scope is required.
- The initiative requires a specific management methodology to be followed.
- The initiative manager and team must identify risk categories to be used and identify at least "n" opportunities and threats for each.

The key here is scalability. Small initiatives lasting a few months may only require an informal agreement to proceed. In contrast, a one-year initiative may require a charter, a methodology, and three to five risks (with a mix of opportunities and threats) to proceed. Reasonable constraints and boundaries help to assure initiative success.

Framework Overview

Integrate the risk management process from the risk assessment framework into the initiative life cycle to analyze and manage opportunities and threats at any time. The primary deliverables are the results produced and documented by a risk assessment workshop (e.g., the risk log, risk assessment workshop report), held during initiative planning, and repeated at selected times throughout the initiative life cycle. Integrate risk management via the framework into initiatives such as operations (e.g., for supply chain risk management) and strategic planning (e.g., for business risk management) to expand usage to enterprise-wide.

The framework, illustrated in figure 2, consists of two significant areas: risk assessment and risk control. Develop a risk plan at the start of risk assessment. Identify and analyze risks in terms of likelihood and impact, and plan responses. Qualitative analysis helps identify the most significant and relevant risks. A shorter list of risks of the highest priorities, those that may need changes in plans or contingency plans, is possible. Planning risk responses may identify new risks, so it is necessary to return to identification to make sure they are appropriately incorporated.

Risk control coincides with initiative execution. Control begins once you are comfortable that there have been enough iterations to provide the best risk log possible. Monitoring starts with scanning the initiative and its environment for risk triggers (i.e., events that signal a risk is about to occur). Implement risk response plans if a risk is imminent or already realized. At this point, there is a return to monitoring. More importantly, there is a need to recognize the initiative is heading down a new path with new opportunities and threats. Once again, there is a need to return to risk assessment to identify and plan for managing unknown risks.

Perform risk assessment for the first time during initiative planning and incorporate it into the overall initiative plan documentation. If thorough, the plan will only require minimal updates unless it becomes necessary to re-plan the initiative. Initial identification, analysis, and response planning are the first steps, but repetition throughout the initiative-executing phase may be required. Risk control activities align with the controlling and executing phase through the feedback loops.

For some initiatives that may be very similar, you may develop checklists or processes to avoid identifying common risks. For example, it is common for organizations purchasing enterprise software packages to buy more functionality than they can absorb in a reasonable time. To counter that, one company developed a five-year, high-level plan for customers, showing their path to success.

Note the act of performing risk assessment upfront is no guarantee or expectation that all risks are identified at that time. As you will find by exploring the diagram and thinking about the process, the risk assessment area is both iterative and recursive.

Iterative, as there will be future points when risk identification needs to occur again, such as when a change to the project is made. For example, one of my projects ran into an issue when an electronic component was swapped out for one much smaller. The larger component was not easy to steal; however, dozens of the smaller ones disappeared.

The framework is recursive since one opportunity or threat may lead to others, such as when performing analysis, risk response planning, risk monitoring, and risk response implementation. For example, as part of risk response implementation, I may bring in a new resource. However, I also have a new risk that the resource may not perform for some reason, such as illness, scheduled time off, or lack of necessary skills.

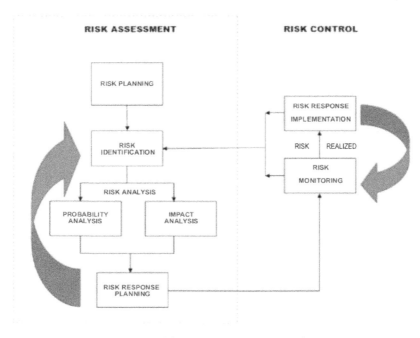

Figure 2. Risk Assessment Framework

Each step of the risk management process has associated inputs, processes, outputs, and critical success factors. Supporting implementation tools, templates, forms, and guidance are in Sections II and III. Section II contains expanded coverage of tailoring the framework, risk management plan, risk assessment workshop, and RAID (risks, actions, issues, decisions) log (an advanced form of risk log). Brief descriptions of other tools and templates are in Section III and may require more investigation and practice before use.

Subsequent chapters in this section document the framework, and each contains five sections:

- Description
- Input
- Process
- Output
- Critical Success Factors

Chapter Summary

- Risks have two major components.
- Risks with favorable or positive impacts are known as "opportunities." Those with unfavorable or adverse effects are known as "threats."
- The risk assessment framework has two major areas: risk assessment and risk control.
- Universal risks are those risks that can occur in any initiative in any industry.
- Understanding the sources of risk and developing categories for them will aid the risk identification process.
- The risk assessment framework is both iterative and recursive.

CHAPTER 2

RISK PLANNING

Description

As a first step, initiate one or more conversations, facilitated meetings, surveys, or other information gathering techniques to determine how the organization will react to risk. For example, consider a company with a 99.999% reliability of network and systems as a goal. The organization aligns compensation, promotion policies, and future employment to these goals to assure everyone and every action supports the goals. There may also be policies and procedures (written and unwritten) in place to ensure goal attainment. There would be a very low tolerance to risks that potentially keep them from meeting the goal.

Tip: Sometimes, attitudes toward risks can be powerful and a part of the organizational culture. It is essential to recognize this for all iterations. For example, let us consider the company with a 99.999% reliability of network and systems as a goal. After a brief discussion about a system bug, a visiting salesperson opened their briefcase, put a tape on the table, and advised them to "just slap it on the system." At that point, management showed the salesperson the door – their handling of system patches went something like this:

- Wait six months
- Call other customers using the same system and find out their experience
- Put the patch on a test system and perform unit and regression testing
- After a QA review, the patch would be scheduled for a release

In addition to the risk profile developed, inputs to risk planning start with the artifacts from initiative initiation, including contracts, statements of work, project/initiative charters, and any other documents available. Additional inputs to risk planning include policies and procedures that are used in organizational and initiative governance. These documents will need review and consideration.

Additional interviews of key initiative participants—such as subject-matter experts and initiative sponsors who may help understand the organization, initiative, and potential risks—might occur. They will be able to provide their expectations and ideas of how risk management should take place. Starting an initial risk log identifies the initial opportunities and threats for use in the next phase. It will be a reference throughout the process.

To complete risk planning, ensure the log—with identified risks, documented customer expectations, and any high-level risk mitigation options —is ready for the next step. The amount of formality in this documentation will depend significantly upon factors such as the following:

- Initiative size: Do we need to provide information about risks to many people?
- Initiative value: Is there a lot at financial risk for the organization?
- Personnel changes: Is there a team dedicated to the process, or will a new team pick up the work?
- Schedule of the initiative: How frequently are reviews required?
- Biases: Do we need to overcome weaknesses in planning and recognition of risks?
- Client/employer expectations for methodology: Are the initiative risk management practices acceptable to all stakeholders? To any involved regulatory or licensing bodies?

Apply these decisions and factors throughout this framework. It is also a given that whatever form the risk management plan is in will be an input to each part of the process.

Inputs

- Contracts, statement of work, initiative charters, and other governance (e.g., policies, procedures, regulations) and initiative documents containing stakeholder requirements
- Risk profile (i.e., a document detailing attitudes toward risk within the organization or initiative, see Section III for details)
- Risk policies (i.e., specific governance documents addressing risks and risk management)

Process

- Review documents.
- Identify and interview select initiative stakeholders for planning input.
- Develop a risk management plan.
- Start a risk log (two templates are included with this book) and update it in each framework step.

Outputs

- Initial risk log with identified opportunities and threats
- A completed risk management plan
- Documented client expectations for risk management

Critical Success Factors

- Completeness of plan and acceptance by stakeholders
- Scale planning to the initiative (e.g., a simple project should probably consume no more than a day to develop the draft risk management plan and risk log)

Chapter Summary

Risk Planning

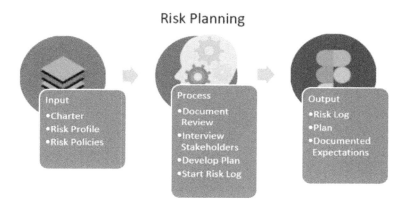

Figure 3: Risk Planning

CHAPTER **3**

RISK IDENTIFICATION

Description

For the risk identification step of the process, start with stakeholder expectations for risk management and candidate risks, and complete the list. Initiative team members participating in the identification need to review all documentation and use various tools and techniques (e.g., facilitated meetings, cause-effect diagrams, force field analysis) to identify as many risks as possible.

 At this point, it is better to overidentify risks rather than miss something significant. It may also be necessary to time-box the identification. There may be considerable risks, so the focus needs to be on those most probable and most impactful risks. Shorten or expand the list as necessary as the process moves forward.

Inputs

- Risk management plan
- Candidate opportunities and threats from initial risk log
- Documented stakeholder expectations for risk management

Process

- Review documentation.
- Use tools such as the following (see implementation guide for complete list and descriptions) to identify risks and add them to the risk log:
    - Risk categories to encourage depth and breadth of thinking
    - Risk assessment workshop / facilitated meetings (e.g., brainstorming)
    - Checklists of risks
    - Cause and effect diagrams and other analytical tools which serve to highlight risks
    - "Risk radar" (e.g., an automated, data-based solution to look for risks[1])

---

[1] When the term "risk radar" was used in the original framework, the idea was simply to monitor a database or set a database trigger to send an email for high value initiatives. Today there are actually products which have trademarked or registered this phrase. Two such products are Pro Concepts Risk Radar® Enterprise (https://proconceptsllc.com/risk-radar-enterprise/) designed for enterprise risk management and Risk Radar™ by Arkus for financial portfolios (https://www.riskradar.com/).

Outputs

- Completed candidate list of opportunities and threats in a risk log

Critical Success Factors

- Comprehensive and early identification of opportunities and threats with high likelihood and impacts on initiatives

Chapter Summary

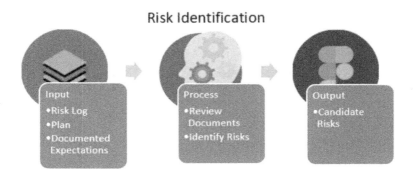

Figure 4: Risk Identification

CHAPTER **4**

RISK ANALYSIS

Description

As a next step, analyze risks to determine their priority (also referred to as severity). Forecast their relative and actual impact on the initiative regarding budget, schedule, quality, and other plans. The priority of risks is essential as initiatives get larger. If the process identifies thousands of risks, it may not be possible to allocate enough time to analyze and determine response strategies for all.

First, start with the candidate risks and perform a thorough analysis to determine the relative likelihood and actual financial and time impact of each risk. For impacts, look at both relative and actual estimated impacts. The relative impacts, along with likelihood, will inform the risk priority. In contrast, the actual impacts will inform the need for modifications to budgets, schedules, and other plans. These modifications are known as contingency reserves. While it may have some shortcomings, one of the simplest ways to compute budget contingency reserves is:

$$CR = \sum_{1}^{n} EMV$$

where:

CR = Contingency Reserve
EMV = Estimated Monetary Value
n = Number of Risks

Equation 1: Contingency Reserve Calculation

A similar computation can identify contingency reserves for schedules using ETV (estimated time value). Further details of these computations are in Section III. Be sure to look at both the hard dollar impact (actual costs) and any soft dollar impact (costs challenging to estimate, such as those generated by goodwill or change in reputation). Perhaps a large amount of money is not at stake. Still, the credibility as an organization is at risk, potentially reducing sales by a large but difficult to estimate amount. While they are not directly added to the reserve, they should be listed in support of the reserve.

Tip: It may not be unusual for some organizations to assign a fixed percentage (typically 5-15%) of the initiative budget for contingency reserves. Good initiative managers will perform the actual computations and review them to avoid surprises later in the initiative.

Tip: Time is money (e.g., money spent on resources). Therefore, I like to consider reserves for schedules and not just budgets.

This same analysis will help support the process of determining risk responses. If the financial impact is small, there is no need to spend a large amount of time on the response. For example, a task threat may be overtime hours payable if the task fails to end on time. Spending more than the overtime pay to crash (add more resources to) the task would not be a financially responsible response.

To be both thorough and efficient, consider splitting the team to perform both analytical steps simultaneously. Have half the team work on probability analysis. In contrast, the other half works on impact, both qualitative (relative impact) and quantitative (estimated actual impact). When each group has completed their analysis, ask them to exchange outputs, and perform a review. Taking this approach will also help reduce the likely bias if everyone must work together on both the probabilities and impacts. If either group finds a new risk, they should record it and provide their analysis portion. When conducting their review, the other group will fill in their part.

Finally, examine the generated data for any trends. Is there perhaps one action that could eliminate or reduce the likelihood or impact of more than one risk? Keep in mind Pareto's Law, which applies here: 80 percent of the effects come from 20 percent of the causes. While this is a very broad-brush, pseudoscientific view, it is still a good rule of thumb.

Subject-matter experts from outside the team need to participate in critical analyses to identify all significant risks. As the old saying goes, we sometimes cannot see the forest for the trees. Any experts not directly participating in the analysis should review and provide feedback on the completed risk log.

Retain all minutes and reports from any analysis meetings. These serve as review materials for the current initiative and form a repository of risk management information for future initiatives. The PMBOK Guide stresses the best practice of maintaining historical documentation. Such documentation may serve many purposes:

- Help a new initiative manager come up to speed
- Help new team members come up to speed in the event of team turnover
- It becomes a reference if looking at past decisions becomes critical to moving forward
- Supplement lessons-learned in historical documents to serve as a basis of guidance for future initiatives which may have similar needs

Inputs

- Risk management plan
- Risk log containing candidate opportunities and threats

Process

- Analyze risks. Use tools such as the following to perform analysis (these are all discussed further in Section III):
  - Risk assessment workshop / facilitated meetings
  - Risk priority number (RPN) from failure modes and effects analysis (FMEA)
  - Risk Assessment Matrix (also known as a probability-impact matrix)
  - Decision tree
  - Simulation
- Determine initial contingency reserves (use of Equation 1 is recommended).

Outputs

- Risk severities updated in the risk log
- Time and cost (and possibly other) impacts updated in the risk log; initial contingency reserves
- Trend analysis (e.g., are there certain risks that are recurring in multiple categories or are closely related in their category)
- Meeting Minutes/Reports

Critical Success Factors

- Use of agreed-upon techniques
- Collection of credible and unbiased risk data and information
- Competence in the application of analytical techniques

Chapter Summary

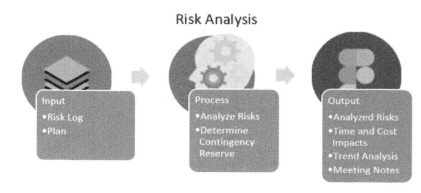

Figure 5: Risk Analysis

CHAPTER **5**

RISK RESPONSE PLANNING

Description

The risk management log and the documentation completed in the process's risk analysis step now form the input for risk response planning. Here there is a need to perform a slightly different kind of brainstorming and analysis. Review each item in more detail and determine the responses to employ.

There may be too many opportunities and threats to respond to them effectively in more complex or riskier initiatives. The previous step (risk analysis) prioritization can play an important role. It should focus on the highest-priority risks to avoid "analysis paralysis" and meet time constraints without adding additional risk or missing any significant risks.

Per the PMBOK Guide, five primary opportunity response strategies and five immediate threat response strategies are suitable for all initiatives. While Section II of this book provides more detailed guidance, the short explanation of each strategy for opportunities (positive risks) and threats (adverse risks) is:

Opportunity

Escalate: Make the organization aware of an opportunity outside of the initiative's scope or our authority, which may benefit the organization or the initiative. A higher level of the organization (e.g., portfolio, program, senior management) manages these opportunities.

Adopt: Take steps to ensure the realization of the benefits of the opportunity.

Enable: Increase the likelihood or impact of the opportunity.

Share: Share some of the benefits with a third party (e.g., form a partnership) to help us assure the realization of benefits.

Accept: Take advantage of the opportunity should it present itself, but do not actively pursue it.

Threat

Escalate: Make the organization aware of a threat outside of the initiative's scope or our authority, which may impact the organization or initiative. A higher level of the organization (e.g., portfolio, program, senior management) manages these threats.

Avoid: Eliminate the threat such that the risk can no longer become an issue.

Accept: Acknowledge the threat will become an issue and take little or no further action. Damage control may be necessary if the threat becomes an issue.

Transfer: Shift the impact of the threat to a third party (e.g., purchase an insurance policy).

Mitigate: Reduce the likelihood or impact of the threat.

It may be necessary to iterate several times to determine the best response strategy. It is also essential to define and specify the risk triggers (events that indicate the risk is about to turn into an issue or benefit). For example, a forecasted, approaching tornado may trigger a construction project to stop work and advise workers to take shelter)—document concrete actions for each trigger. Measures may include performing a risk-benefit analysis for high-cost items.

Response planning may result in the need for further adjustment to the budget and time contingency reserves. Budgets and timelines may need an increase (or decrease) to cover the impact of an identified, known risk. For example, suppose the cost of the final, agreed-upon response to a threat is greater than the estimated effects. In that case, the contingency reserve may need an increase. It is also possible that due to a response, a risk may likely be decreased in impact, in which case the budgets and timelines may need a decrease.

The final output of risk response planning is the completed log, accompanying analysis, and risk responses. Once more, the amount of detail may change based on the size of the initiative. For substantial, complex initiatives, which may take place in diverse and distant locations, the initiative manager obviously cannot be everywhere and watching everything. It is common in large initiatives for the initiative manager to identify and empower specific team members to be risk owners. Risk owners act using the agreed-upon response plans if the likelihood or impact of risk increases past a certain threshold or a risk trigger occurs.

Inputs

- Risk management plan
- Risk log
- Completed analysis documents with any preliminary responses

Process

- Determine response strategy (opportunity: escalate, adopt, enable, share, accept; threat: escalate, avoid, accept, transfer, mitigate).
- Formulate response plans, perform risk-benefit analysis for significant items, and calculate final recommended contingency reserves; include the documentation's risk triggers.
- Review changes made to initiative plans by response plans (loop back to risk identification).

Outputs

- Revised log and analysis
- Risk responses (including triggers, documented in risk log)
- Final contingency reserves to update budgets and timelines

Critical Success Factors

- Stakeholder buy-in to response plans
- An accurate specification of risk triggers, response timing, resources, budgets, and schedules
- Follow a risk response process to reduce bias and assure better decision-making.

Risk Response Planning

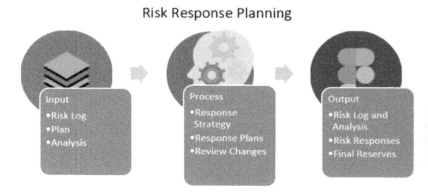

Figure 6: Risk Response Planning

CHAPTER 6

RISK MONITORING

Description

As the initiative moves into execution, risk monitoring needs to be in place. Risk monitoring scans the environment for risk triggers. These events indicate the risk is going to become a benefit or an issue. Finding the trigger may be a matter of discussion, observation, or data collection (e.g., metrics) and review. When detecting a trigger, monitoring passes control to risk response implementation to reduce the impact or probability of risk or avoid the risk altogether. The inputs to this process include the risk log, risk management plan, the documentation created in previous steps of the framework, and the documentation, which has evolved from the initiative planning process.

Some good ways to conduct the process of monitoring are as follows:

- Have periodic reviews[2]. The reviews should consider the following questions:
    - Is the approach to risk management still appropriate for this initiative; is it followed?
    - Has the overall level of initiative risk changed?
    - Are there new opportunities or threats now present?
    - Are risk triggers observed?
    - Are the response strategies selected still sound?
    - Were responses deployed as planned, and were they effective?
    - Are the previously established budget and time reserves still appropriate?
    - Are the right people responsible for managing risks?
- Track the risk log as part of status reporting. Management reports will typically emphasize the top critical risks and issues, track all items, and make them available for team review. Tracking is the responsibility of the initiative manager or their designee.
- Review key performance indicators or other initiative-generated data to uphold thresholds.

Tip: Good prioritization by computing the severity (probability x impact) is essential because it is usually not practical to monitor or review every risk regularly. Focus on those with high priorities within the period you are studying. It is often adequate for the initiative manager to check the others at a longer interval (e.g., once a month). Sort the risks such that the highest severity risks are

---

[2] Top priority risks for the normal performance period of an initiative should be reviewed (e.g., a project has a weeky status meeting; during that meeting the top risks for the period are reviewed). All other risks should be regularly reviewed by the initiative manager, typically every month or two.

always at the top of the list, and the least severity risks are at the bottom.

The process's output is the updated plans, logs, status reports, and other documentation updates.

Inputs

- Risk management plan
- Risk log
- Initiative planning, performance, and status documentation (budget, status reports, schedules, etc.), including metrics

Process

- Hold periodic reviews – focus on priority risks for the current period.
- Track risks as part of status/performance reporting.
- Ensure manual or automated review of initiative metrics.

Outputs

- Plans, risk log, status reports, and other documentation with updates as appropriate
- Any observations or data collected by monitoring

Critical Success Factors

- Maintaining continuous awareness of the initiative environment
- Thorough and complete risk log

Chapter Summary

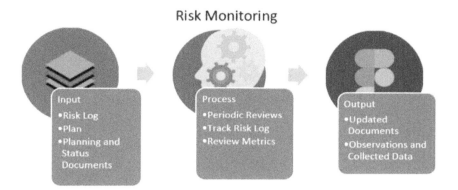

Figure 7: Risk Monitoring

CHAPTER 7

RISK RESPONSE IMPLEMENTATION

Description

Finally, the risk response implementation step takes the plan, log, and response plans as input. Implement response plans as necessary to navigate opportunities and threats. Be sure any opportunity or threat having a high likelihood and high impact is already under consideration or previously implemented. Review and revise plans, logs, and other documentation as necessary to document the implementation.

When this step of the process is complete, monitoring must continue. Also, because a risk response has changed the initiative's course, there is a need to return to risk identification. This ensures the actions have introduced no new opportunities or threats. Route any new opportunities or threats through the process and add them to the plans; this is a critical step.

Inputs

- Risk management plan
- Risk log
- Risk response plans
- Observations or data collected by monitoring

Process

- Implement the proactively agreed-upon response plans when and as needed.
- Ensure any risk high in both likelihood and impact has actions already under consideration.

Outputs

- Revised log, plans

Critical Success Factors

- Thoroughness of planning
- Clear, honest, transparent, and unbiased communication about risks
- An agreed-upon, empowered owner responsible for the implementation
- A return to risk identification to determine if there are new opportunities or threats.

Chapter Summary

Risk Response Implementation

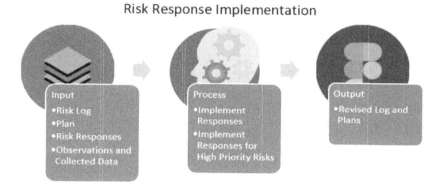

Figure 8: Risk Response Implementation

SECTION II: ACHIEVING SUCCESS WITH THE RISK ASSESSMENT FRAMEWORK

"What you have to do and the way you have to do it is incredibly simple. Whether you are willing to do it is another matter."

— Peter Drucker

CHAPTER 8

INTRODUCTIONS TO SUCCESSFUL IMPLEMENTATIONS

Create an Environment for Success

The nature of the working environment is vital to a successful implementation. Environmental factors to consider include:

- The current state of the organization
- Attitudes toward risk and risk management (are they positive or negative?)
- Support for innovation
- Communications

To create an environment for success, first study the current state of the organization. Is there a risk management process in place for initiatives? Does management support the process? Has it been successful? Speak with initiative managers and other stakeholders in the organization. Review policies and procedures, then document findings.

Many organizations are subject to what is known as the "Titanic Effect" (Cook 2010). They consider themselves too large and invulnerable to fail and do not consider the uncertainties their initiatives may need to navigate. Such organizations usually have little or no regard for risk management processes. Consider collecting data about risks and their impacts over time. The collected data will enable you to support risk management through a calculated return on investment (ROI) and a business case.

For one of my earliest software projects, I focused almost exclusively on opportunities and innovation. The project plan included tasks and activities such as:

- Getting the best team in place – everyone from regular staff to our intern wanted to work on the project
- Designing standard interfaces first, which the whole team would use, to prevent unnecessary change later in the project
- Finding and re-purposing existing code significantly reduced the overall effort
- Benchmarking key algorithms – we knew there would be some challenges to our methods, but when they came, we had the data to support them
- Identifying the early adopters and supporters for our project and working with them first to get assistance in getting everyone else on board

As a result of these and other identified opportunities, we completed the project in one year, with high quality, and with a team of four full-time team members and one summer intern. Other companies were taking upwards of five years and teams double or triple the size of ours to do the same projects.

On the other hand, at least five organizations in my past failed to manage critical and mostly predictable threats appropriately. As a result, they failed themselves. Their costs due to these threats included:

- 45 of 50 multi-million dollar sales going to a competitor as unmitigated uncertainty held up initiative completion
- Failure to manage "payment in kind" (e.g., trade for goods and services as payment) as opposed to cash payments led to unrecoverable costs
- After a growth spurt, ignored uncertainty led to a significant contraction; continuously ignoring the problem, a second contraction occurred
- 100% debt-funded company creating a single product failed after being unable to sell the product
- An avoidable $600K loss of materials by a failure of senior management to communicate a project change

Very often, a small amount of time spent to embrace high benefit opportunities or stop major and predictable threats can pay for itself. Scan the organizational environment to see if there have been past or current incidents and use them to present a business case for risk management. Recommend how to move from the current situation to something improved, with a well-thought-out and supported process. Use this to get buy-in from senior executives for strengthening risk management.

It is also necessary to communicate effectively about risk. Focus on those highest in priority and do not over-or under-play any risks. Open and transparent communication about risk will help everyone get more comfortable with the topic of risk. Resist "sweeping problems under rugs" or declaring issues about threats as unwanted.

Tip: Be sure to consider risks when you develop the communication plan for your initiatives.

Suppose there is limited support for risk management (I have worked with organizations where leadership does not want to discuss anything "negative" or waste time on risk management). In that case, it will take some time to change the organization. One of the best ways to begin this type of change is through conversations and questions. Consider periodically raising some of these questions in discussions about initiatives as appropriate:

- What are the consequences if the initiative fails?
- Are we able to spare a half-day to ensure initiative success?
- Are there any opportunities and threats we should be aware of as we begin the initiative?
- How do the stakeholders feel about risks and the initiative?
- Are we confident the scope and all assumptions of the initiative are well defined?
- Suppose we do not use an appropriate risk management method. How will we identify the proper contingencies for the budget and timeline of the initiative?
- Are there any business or cultural issues within the organization that could affect the success of the initiative?
- What is the tolerance for risk for the organization overall and within specific stakeholder groups in the organization?

Tip: The initiative manager must understand the organization's actual position, which may not be totally against or for risk management. Most executives want a positive, "can-do" attitude, so do not expect that risk management is an exercise to compile excuses for later failures.

Implementing the risk assessment framework over time will also set the organization up for success. Successful navigation of uncertainty begins as soon as the process starts. First, try it out "as is" or with only a few modifications. Add to the process with future initiatives to create a robust process.

An Implementation Checklist

Use this brief checklist to guide the activities necessary to successfully implement the risk assessment framework, including planning and conducting a risk assessment workshop. It is not meant to be prescriptive; however, it enumerates the elements needed to implement the framework successfully. Keep in mind that every action may need to be scaled or tailored for your organization.

- ❑ Read and become familiar with the risk assessment framework.
- ❑ Read this section (Achieving Success with the Risk Assessment Framework)
- ❑ Decide if there will be any modifications to the framework. It is not necessary yet; make changes later after there is some experience with the framework. Electronic copies of the Sources of Risk: A Taxonomy chart, the framework-process diagram, and many other tools and templates to help document and support modifications (see Appendix B: License to Use and Modify Templates and Instructional Materials) are available.
- ❑ Complete a Risk Management plan using the provided template. A well-constructed plan will be able to serve many initiatives within the organization.
- ❑ Review the provided risk log templates and make any necessary adjustments or modifications.
- ❑ Plan the first risk assessment workshop.

- o Review and modify the risk categories (Sources of Risk) as necessary.
- o Interview significant stakeholders to create a risk profile.
- o Prefill the risk log for the initiative based on interview results (all supplied templates include pre-filled examples).
- o Determine facilitation techniques for each meeting segment (see Section III of this book); conduct segment identification, analysis, and risk response planning.
- o Complete and distribute an agenda (using the supplied template).
- o Conduct the workshop.
- o Complete the risk assessment workshop report (template available).
- ❑ Collect and review detailed risk response plans.
- ❑ Provide regular status reports on critical opportunities and threats; regularly review the risk log.
- ❑ Conduct a risk "lessons-learned" session at the end of the initiative to determine what might need improvement for the next one. Review the risk management plan, risk log, and risk assessment workshop documents. However, they should require limited or no modification.

Already have a risk management process in place? Then review and compare the implementation checklist, tools, and techniques to current practices. The review may yield some process improvements.

Risk management processes, tools, and techniques are not just a part of initial planning. Use them effectively in other situations such as:

- During project initiation activities as part of sizing, costing, and proposal generation
- When assuming responsibility for a program or project already in progress
- In "runaway systems" recovery
- During major plan revisions
- When significant deviations from the plan occur

Also, use these same processes to uncover and mitigate opportunities and threats in business planning, financial planning, and operations management. They apply to any initiative.

The Importance of Continuous Improvement

Getting started is more important when dealing with uncertainty than being perfect. The framework is sufficiently complete, so it is possible to start with it "as is", if necessary, and perform tailoring later. Simple brainstorming with the right experts and stakeholders is usually adequate for a first risk assessment workshop. Consider making sure the workshop gets in place sooner rather than later – this statistically increases the chances of initiative success.

Continuous improvement is about making ongoing improvements to products, services, and processes. The most widely used tool for continuous improvement is the four-step model, sometimes known as the Deming or Shewhart Cycle. The four-step model checks the efficiency of a change on a small scale before full-scale implementation. Base the decision to move to full-scale implementation on data.

The four-step model is also referred to as Plan-Do-Check-Act (PDCA). PDCA is based on the scientific method: hypothesis – experiment – evaluation (ASQ 2021). An essential aspect of PDCA is the careful separation of each step, without overlap. Perform each step thoughtfully, carefully, and confirm step outcomes before proceeding to the next stage. This level of care helps guide the thinking and ensure the integrity of the process. Do not start "Do" until a solid "Plan" is in place.

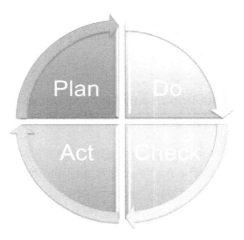

Figure 9: Plan-Do-Check-Act Model

The iteration is equally essential. Each cycle brings us more knowledge and closer to a perfect risk management process, making PDCA a vital tool in avoiding "analysis paralysis." We can test our observations, guesses, and assumptions on a small scale before full commitment.

The steps in detail include:

Plan: Collect and study performance data to identify an improvement.

Do: Make a small, incremental improvement first, and …

Check: that the change was effective.

Act: Once verified, move toward full implementation.

Here are a few small changes I have identified over the years that are important to consider while moving forward and improving the risk management method:

- Connect any risk response actions with business strategies and priorities and align the responses with the risk response strategies.
- Consider if there should be some goals to identify specific numbers of opportunities.
- Consider how to avoid group-think and cognitive biases present in risk assessment workshops.
- Constraints are typically associated with risks (e.g., will we exceed them?) and need to be included in identification.

It is easier to navigate the uncertainties of future initiatives by adopting a mindset of continuous improvement. Initiatives will continue to deliver improved benefits more efficiently to the organization.

Tip: Many organizations will schedule an annual "improvement" project designed to boost employee and initiative productivity. Consider if there is an opportunity to insert one or more PDCA improvements in it.

- The process of risk management needs a supportive environment to succeed. You can create that environment by:
  - Studying the current state of the organization
  - Developing support for innovation and open communications
  - Trying a focus on opportunities for their positive effect
  - Asking questions to lead organizational change
- Use the supplied implementation checklist to guide the framework implementation.
- Getting started is an essential first step – adopt a mindset of continuous improvement to make small improvements iteratively.
- Plan-Do-Check-Act (PDCA) is a suitable method for implementing continuous improvement.

CHAPTER 9

TAILORING THE FRAMEWORK

Introduction

Nearly every process step of the framework can benefit from tailoring to personalize it and scale it for the organization. As with any changes, planning and analysis are necessities.

Small-to-medium-sized initiatives were considerations when developing the framework, so it is possible to try it out "as is" first for these types of initiatives. This chapter examines the steps of the framework in more detail and identifies the critical decisions to consider. The step descriptions refer to tools and techniques available to support the framework. These and other tools and methods are described in more detail in Section III, Tools and Techniques Supporting the Risk Assessment Framework.

In general, begin with a review of the framework steps, make some tentative decisions for each step, and move forward. There is no need to aim for immediate perfection. Precision in risk management will come over time through continuous improvement. It is more important to begin by planning to embrace significant opportunities and avoid catastrophic and critical threats. These will provide an immediate return on the investment of time and expense.

A reasonable first implementation is to identify an initiative (project-level recommended) that will benefit from risk assessment. Commence the planning, and then schedule a risk assessment workshop. Do a team walk-through, so they understand how to tailor and implement the process. The workshop, which may range from a few hours to a few days long (depending on the initiative's size and scope), should facilitate identifying significant risks through risk response planning.

Risk Planning

A vital tool for implementing the risk assessment framework is a risk assessment workshop (RAW), which carries out the framework process steps from risk identification through risk response planning. Before conducting the RAW, complete a risk management plan.

For risk planning, the critical question to answer is, "How much planning and management is enough?" There is no immediate answer to this question; however, start with the primary recommendations of the framework and this book and use continuous improvement to home in on the best solution. The goal is to provide enough risk management such that:

- Costs and time of implementing risk management are proportionate to the initiatives' costs and time. Less than 10% is a good starting figure.

- Identified vital opportunities generate benefits, potentially offsetting the negative impact of threats.
- Plans avoid or proactively mitigate critical and catastrophic risks.
- The plan puts the team in control to proactively manage risks.
- Key metrics measure the success of risk management and establish the groundwork for continuous improvement.
- Any major initiative requires a RAW to identify, analyze, and plan mitigation responses for high-priority risks.

The goal of the framework and this book is to reduce overhead and delays. Newly collected metrics as the process moves forward may require a further change in the future.

Another critical part of planning is identifying the roles and responsibilities of the RAW and overall risk management process participants. Start with the following table and modify or expand as necessary:

Roles	Responsibilities
Initiative Sponsor/Senior Management	• Ensure the success of multiple related initiatives. • Ensure initiatives are following policies and methodologies, including risk management • Clear organizational hurdles and provide necessary resources. • Participate in risk assessment workshops and periodic reviews as required. • Make decisions and take necessary actions to address escalated risks.

	• Sign off on high-impact risks.
	• Agree to the implementation of risk response plans.
Initiative Manager or Lead	• Determine stakeholders' attitudes toward risk.
	• Engage initiative sponsor/senior management in the process.
	• Tailor the framework with stakeholder inputs.
	• Lead the development of the risk management plan.
	• Schedule the workshops and document their outcomes.
	• Facilitate the assignment of risk owners (or personally assume the role for smaller initiatives).
	• Update budgets, timelines, and other planning documents, as necessary, with risk response plans.
	• Maintain the risk log.
	• Escalate risks as appropriate (e.g., if there is no consensus on risk response or when the risk is out of team control).
	• Document team escalation processes.
	• Validate and act on newly identified risks throughout the initiative.
	• Monitor and control the process; lead periodic reviews.
	• Monitor the effectiveness of the risk assessment framework.
	• Collect and act on lessons learned.
Initiative Manager or Facilitator	• Ensure conditions are right to begin the workshop.
	• Facilitate the risk assessment workshop impartially.
	Be sure all team members have a voice.

	• Be sensitive to any financial, contractual, political, or personnel issues that are not appropriate in a public forum and address these separately with proper stakeholders. • Ensure there are no time pressures, but allow the workshop to conclude when the team agrees identification is complete. • Document the workshop outcomes.
Business Analyst	• Collaborate with the initiative manager to identify organizational tolerance and appetite for risk. • Reduce threats and maximize opportunities using requirements eliciting, documenting, and tracing best practices. • Assist in the identification of risks (opportunities and threats) related to the recommended solution. • Potentially fill a risk owner role or other team member role for business issues and solution risks.
Risk Owner(may be the initiative manager/ designated lead for smaller initiatives)	• Participate in risk assessment workshops and periodic reviews as required. • Develop detailed response plans for assigned risks. • Track assigned risks. • Recommend preventive actions designed to take full advantage of opportunities or prevent or reduce threat likelihood and impacts. • Implement response plans when the risk event/trigger does occur. • Monitor the effectiveness of all actions taken for assigned risks.

| Initiative Team Member | • Participate in risk assessment workshops and periodic reviews as required. |
| | • Document newly found risks and submit them to the initiative manager for validation and action. |

Table 1: Risk Assessment Framework Roles and Responsibilities

In the framework, we talk a bit about the tolerance and opinions of risk the project stakeholders may have. Culture may also play a significant role in international teams. And we also need to recognize that all organizations have a culture, regardless of their locale.

Figure 10: Busy Jakarta Street During Rush Hour

Take a close look at the picture taken on a busy Jakarta street during rush hour. See the tiny feet between mom and dad on the motorbike? How many parents in North America would feel comfortable riding this way (no helmet for mom or child)? Dad is just wearing sandals, and it is too hot and expensive for protective outerwear. It is not unusual to see a family of five (or more) with one child standing on the front platform, a mom with a baby, and more children riding between parents.

To the people that travel this way daily, this is the norm and not as risky for them as we might imagine it. So, as you move forward in an international project, be sure you ask enough questions to understand the local concepts of risk.

Risk Identification

Risk identification needs to happen early and often. At the start of any project, review the project charter, and discuss with the project sponsor. Were any risks identified during the chartering process? Get these into the risk log and be prepared to share them during the risk assessment workshop's initial hours. It is also good to consider past initiatives – learn from past mistakes.

Risk identification is the first step of the risk assessment workshop. Here the team identifies the opportunities and threats which may impact the initiative.

Conduct one or more facilitated meetings using brainstorming and other idea generation techniques to identify risks. Descriptions of a rich set of techniques for facilitating risk identification are in the next section, along with their strengths and weaknesses. Browse through them and determine which ones will work best for the current organization and initiative.

The Sources of Risk: A Taxonomy chart of the framework is a source document to introduce risks and set expectations for identification. Review this taxonomy periodically. Suppose too many risks consistently fall into one category. In that case, it may be a sign to add a new category, or there are other organizational or initiative issues to examine.

The PMBOK Guide includes similar ideas to establish categories: prompt lists compiled from some common strategic frameworks. One closely related to the taxonomy is PESTLE analysis, which includes political, economic, social, technological, legal, and environmental categories (PMI 2017).

Make sure your identification carefully and clearly describes the risk. It may help to include some words from the category to indicate the origin. For example, rather than state "over budget," write "client merger and acquisition may cause budget overrun."

Use the provided Risk Profile template to collect initial thoughts and inputs from initiative stakeholders as necessary before the risk assessment workshop. Use these as a starter list of risks to get ideas flowing.

Over the years, I have found opportunities are the most difficult to identify, especially when trying to do so simultaneously with threats. Consider the following possibilities to improve opportunity identification:

- Create two prompt lists: one for opportunities and another for threats. Consider them in separate sessions.
- Use different brainstorming forms (identified in Section III) such as Brainswarming®, Six Thinking Hats, or Appreciative Inquiry as they can help orient mindsets.

- Include and encourage more creative team members to contribute.
- Challenge the team to generate a risk log with at least 20% opportunities.
- Break and steer the team toward opportunities when thinking is too pessimistic.
- Try "flipping" negatives into positives (e.g., if a risk for an event going over budget, think about the opportunity to allow for sponsorships to provide additional funding).

Organizations with technology support may want to consider the use of programmatic means (also referred to as "risk radar"). For example, the organization may maintain a database of initiatives, using a database trigger to flag those over $X (or with other parametric characteristics) for requiring a risk assessment.

Tip: It is often better to over-identify risks rather than identifying too few. After identification, make a pass over the list of identified risks and remove duplicates and consolidate those that may be similar.

Risk Analysis

Risk analysis is the second topic the team tackles in a risk assessment workshop. Risk identification and risk analysis are two independent efforts. Failure to maintain this separation allows bias to have an impact on the analysis. Consider adding resources (e.g., subject matter experts) to the team for risk analysis. Those who participated in the identification will be available to explain what they had in mind. At the same time, those new to the team will keep an open mind, identify additional risks, and be more objective in their analysis.

Risk analysis usually involves three significant steps:

1) probability analysis to determine the relative likelihood of the risk
2) impact analysis to determine the relative impact of risk
3) impact analysis to determine the estimated actual impact (note for many smaller, more straightforward initiatives, the first two steps may be enough)

A primary goal of risk analysis is the prioritization of risks. Risk analysis combines the likelihood of the risk with the relative impact to determine the priority of risks. A second goal, especially for larger and more complex initiatives, is to determine the estimated cost and time impact of the risks. Having this information means:

1) When considering risk responses, the response's risk-benefit and time impact will help ensure the response is both financially responsible and efficient to implement.
2) The cost and time impacts will inform contingencies needed for budgets and schedules.

To avoid bias, consider having two independent groups performing the probability and impact analysis. While the framework shows the analyses occurring in parallel, some organizations may focus on one ahead of the other. Still, others may add analysis of additional factors, such as:

- The difficulty in determining if a risk trigger will or has happened (also referred to as detectability)
- Where the risk exists within the initiative output and if there are other risks related to it

- The initiative phase at which the risk exists and if there are other risks at this stage or phase
- The manageability and controllability of the risk
- Connections between related risks
- Impact on strategic goals and objectives

For example, it is common for manufacturing operations to add a risk's relative detectability as the third factor for analysis. Another factor is perfectly acceptable. It helps to refine the risk's priority, and the combined result (relative likelihood, impact, and detectability) will pass to the next framework step. Document the specifics in the risk log for future reference.

Like risk identification, risk analysis is often based on expert knowledge and relies on brainstorming techniques. So, review the methods of risk identification and determine which will work best for the organization.

There are many practical tools in the next section that may provide more objective support for combining the probability and impact analyses. These tools include using quadratic formulas to improve risk prioritization and decision trees and frameworks to support estimates and decision-making related to time and cost.

Tip: Do not ignore challenges to quantifying risks. Make sure to qualitatively analyze every risk for at least likelihood and impact, then focus on those with the highest priority. Work with the team to research existing data or collect new data to aid quantitative analysis.

Risk Response Planning

Risk response planning is the final topic the team will tackle in a risk assessment workshop. After a thorough review of the outputs of risk analysis, appropriate plans must be selected to respond to risks and enable the embracing of opportunities. Once again, the initial risk response planning activities are best determined through strategic planning or brainstorming sessions conducted as part of the risk assessment workshop. Larger initiatives and organizations may assign a risk owner first to a series of risks; then, the risk owner will be responsible for working on the risk response. Choose the technique(s) that work best for the environment.

It is crucial to align the developed responses:

- to the response strategies (e.g., do not make significant changes to plans for an accepted risk)
- to the risk profile of the organization (e.g., in a risk-averse organization, do not allow big risk-taking within responses)
- to the strategies and priorities of the organization (e.g., do not mitigate business risk by suggesting a radically new line of business not related to current business objectives)

There are five significant categories of response to opportunities (we will consider threats separately here) to consider:

1. Adopt the opportunity by taking steps such as:
   a. Adding the opportunity entirely into scope and plans.
   b. Prioritizing functionality (with the customer or sponsor).
   c. Adjusting time, scope, cost, or quality plans as appropriate and with any necessary approvals.

2. Enable the opportunity (increase likelihood, impact, or both) by taking steps such as:
    a. Adding the opportunity entirely into scope and plans after further analysis and refinement.
    b. Prioritizing functionality (with the customer, sponsor, or both).
    c. Removing risky items from the scope, cost, schedule, or quality plans as appropriate and with any necessary approvals.
3. Share the opportunity by taking steps such as:
    a. Forming a partnership or consortium where the partner brings critical skills and knowledge to help realize the benefit.
    b. Hiring an expert who will also share in the benefits of the opportunity.
4. Accept the opportunity and implement it if it requires little or no effort. For example, a vendor informs you of a special discount they will apply to your purchase of electrical fixtures and tiles.
5. Escalate an opportunity outside the initiative's scope, the initiative manager's authority, or both to a higher authority, such as:
    a. A program or portfolio manager
    b. Senior management
    c. The C-suite (e.g., CEO, CIO, CFO)

There are five significant categories of response to threats to consider:

1. Avoid the threat by taking steps such as:
    a. Reducing/de-scoping requirements.
    b. Defining requirements more thoroughly.
    c. Prioritizing functionality (with customer or initiative sponsor).

    d. Adjusting time, scope, cost, or quality plans as appropriate and with any necessary approvals.

2. Accept the threat with little or no further consideration or action. An event occurrence may require corrective action. For example, we may accept a weather risk of a snow day in San Diego due to its temperate climate. Still, in the unlikely event that it does, we may have to accept that time and other project resources may be lost.

3. Transfer the threat or a portion of the threat impact by taking steps such as:
    a. Procuring insurance, including self-insurance.
    b. Hiring an expert.
    c. The initiative funds 50 percent of the contingency, and the customer supports the other 50 percent.
    d. Forming a partnership or consortium where each participant shares an agreed-upon portion of any gain or loss.

4. Mitigate the threat through a focus on actions to minimize impacts and probabilities. Consider steps such as:
    a. Reducing the likelihood by:
        i. Prototyping, scaling, or modeling the requirements/solution.
        ii. Checking references of solution partners.
        iii. Ensuring adequate training and certification of personnel.
        iv. Relying on proven technology.
        v. Undertaking more detailed planning, such as estimating, budgeting, and scheduling.
        vi. Developing a Monte Carlo simulation to predict outcomes based on actions.
    b. Reducing the impact by:
        i. Developing a parallel alternative solution where the cost/benefit is more appropriate.

ii. Decoupling related items—that is, reducing the dependency of one resource on another.

iii. Including a contingency amount in the budget (only drawn on for issues).

5. Escalate a threat that is outside the initiative's scope, the initiative manager's authority, or both to a higher authority within the organization, such as:

   a. A program or portfolio manager
   b. Senior management
   c. The C-suite (e.g., CEO, CIO, CFO)

Suppose the response is to mitigate or transfer the risk. The next step is to identify the responses and triggers, identify actions to carry them out, assign risk owners, and establish response time frames. Also, identify requirements for any contingency time or money. The person, business unit, or organization to which a risk may be transferred must accept the risk to be successful. Consider factors such as whether the new owner of the risk can mitigate the risk; if not, the risk may still occur and impact the initiative.

Suppose the response is to accept or avoid the risk. In that case, it still may be necessary to develop a contingency plan to ensure the strategy will be successful—especially if accepting the risk. Now would be a good time to sort the log or otherwise move the accepted risks to a separate area to focus on the priority risks. The initiative manager may look over this list from time-to-time to determine if there is a need to move any risks to a higher priority.

How do we know when threats should be avoided? Threat avoidance is one area we need to understand more fully. There are many different instances where threats should be avoided altogether. Can we afford to display a priceless work of art in a public place without a security system or adequate insurance?

Probably not – the loss would be more than most individuals could bear. Are the odds against us? If so, we should probably avoid the threat. Some other general times when risks should be considered for avoidance include:

- The probability of occurrence is relatively high, and we are unable to identify effective risk response plans.
- If there are too many alternatives, we should narrow down the choices. More diligence in exploring pros, cons, and benefits may be required to help us get the options to a more reasonable number.
- If we have not identified the benefits of our actions.
- If there is insufficient data.
- If the action does not support a strategic objective of our project or organization.

Suppose the response is to adopt, enable, or share the opportunity. In that case, the next step is to develop the opportunity plan, like mitigating or transferring risk. Any intended partners must provide the expertise required to realize the intended benefits of the opportunity.

It is usual for initiatives with large numbers of risks to not complete response planning for all. Be sure the risk plan defines the threshold (as derived from the risk profile) at which this might occur. Some organizations may want to be sure all highest severity risks are avoided or escalated. Sort the lowest priority risks to the bottom of the log.

Tip: Some organizations and risk managers suggest moving the lowest severity risks to another area or list. Having two lists may have the unfortunate effect of missing a risk with a changing priority. One list is better –sort the low priorities to the bottom of the list.

Once the response strategies and choices are identified, they should also be analyzed for cost and time impacts. A risk-benefit analysis will make sure the responses align with the risks and their effects (for example, we do not want to have to break a dozen eggs to detect an issue with our egg production). Suppose the cost of mitigation is greater than the impact's cost. In that case, it may be necessary to either consider additional solutions or to increase the contingency reserve by the difference.

As risk response planning completes, a good picture of all the impacts on the initiative in terms of budget, cost, and resources will emerge. Update overall plans accordingly. For example, adding the negative impacts of threats and subtracting the positive impacts of opportunities will provide a calculated contingency reserve. See Equation 1 and Section III for more detail. While organizations may allocate a percentage of the budget, the estimated reserve can be valuable later during initiative execution.

The second form of reserve, management reserves, is needed to cover the impacts of "unknown unknowns", the risks not identified in the risk management process. The amount typically ranges from 5-15% of the initiative budget. While contingency reserves may be computed from risk analysis data, as already pointed out, management may assign a percentage of the budget. A calculated contingency reserve larger than arbitrarily assigned contingency reserves may be a signal to increase the management reserve percentage.

As a final step to completing risk response planning, assign a risk owner for each opportunity or threat. This role is responsible for

- tracking, implementing any preventive/facilitative actions (designed to assure benefit realization of an opportunity or to prevent or mitigate the threat occurring),

- implementing mitigation or contingency plans when the risk does happen, and
- monitoring the effectiveness of all actions taken regarding the risk.

There must also be a defined and documented escalation process for opportunities and threats in the overall initiative plan.

Risk Monitoring

The risk monitoring step is a continuous process to determine whether the triggers for risk events are present. Because the risk trigger implies a possible need for change to the initiative environment, this step usually leads the team back to risk identification and assessment to determine new risks. The risk assessment framework processes are repeated to reconsider already- identified risks for any necessary changes to their analysis, responses, or both.

Risk monitoring may drive the need to collect data for initiatives. For example, if weather is vital to work (e.g., in the fields of construction or agriculture), collect weather forecast data to inform of a pending risk trigger. Another example is quality–if high quality is a goal, quality processes will need to collect data about defects.

Risk monitoring is typically handled by periodic risk reviews, which may occur as part of the regular initiative status review. Reviewing dozens or more risks with the entire team is not a good use of time. Each review should focus on the top five to ten priority risks associated with the current period's activities.

The review key points include:

1. Is a risk is occurring (and possibly indicated by data)?
2. Are the "in progress" risk response plans and actions effective?
3. Are any changes affecting the current risk priority as determined by risk analysis (e.g., likelihood and relative impact)?
4. Are any significant changes in the plans (including any assumptions, constraints, actions, and decisions) creating new risks (and a need to re-visit risk identification)?
5. Are the policies, processes, and procedures for risk management followed?
6. Are the contingency and management reserves still enough?

Based on the review results, the initiative manager has a responsibility to update the risk log, risk plans, and other related documentation as required.

During this monitoring step, previously unknown risks, the "unknown unknowns," are more likely to present themselves. Be sure to enter them, tag them as such appropriately, and thoroughly document them in the risk log. Having gone through the risk assessment workshop, a strategy for dealing with the new opportunity or threat was likely part of the discussion. This will make dealing with the benefit or issue easier.

Tip: If using adaptive (iterative, incremental, or agile) methodologies for projects (e.g., Scrum), briefly review the highest priority risks related to the project life cycle and development processes at the start of each iteration.

It may take time to address risks once they become issues (or benefits). While addressing them, more may occur. It is essential at this point to continue to address them in priority order. Maintaining a single log documenting risks throughout their lifecycle is critical. Each reporting period, make sure the risks most relevant for the period are still valid, correctly prioritized, and have reasonable response strategies and action plans.

Risk Response Implementation

If an identified risk occurs, the designated risk owner, possibly in conjunction with the initiative manager, will authorize the proactively identified risk response plans. This action may involve seeking senior management approval to implement the agreed-plans or relying on the risk owners to complete the implementation. The initiative manager is responsible for updating the documentation output from risk response planning. However, the exact actions carried out will most likely vary from initiative-to-initiative. They will be managed as documented in the agreed risk management plan and risk log.

Implementing these plans may lead to the identification of more risks or affect the likelihood or impact of other (already identified) risks. In this case, there should be a new round of risk identification. This step also leads back to risk monitoring; the risk control cycle repeats.

Review the effectiveness of mitigation and contingency actions after their implementation. The result is that the organization may develop checklists of potential risks and develop standard responses to them to be available for future initiatives.

- While it is possible to use the framework "as is", tailor it to meet your organization's needs and initiatives over time.
- Focus on a risk assessment workshop (RAW) to meet the needs of risk identification, risk analysis, and risk response planning.
- Each step of the framework can be tailored (use critical questions for each step):
  1. Risk Planning – How much planning is enough? What are our goals and metrics? What are the roles and responsibilities we need? How does culture impact the perception of risks?
  2. Risk Identification – What categories will we use? How will we facilitate information collection?
  3. Risk Analysis – How will we prioritize risks? What analytical techniques will we use? How will we identify impacts on costs and time?
  4. Risk Response Planning – What strategies for a response do we need? How will we align responses to strategy? How will we assign risk owners?
  5. Risk Monitoring – How will we know when risk triggers occur? What data do we need to collect? How often should we review risks?
  6. Risk Response Implementation – Do our responses create new risks? Are there changes to projects which can uncover unknown risks? How successful are we at proactively addressing risks?

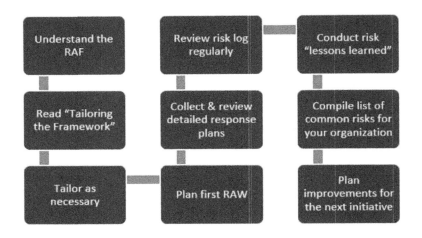

Figure 11: Implementing the Risk Assessment Framework (RAF)

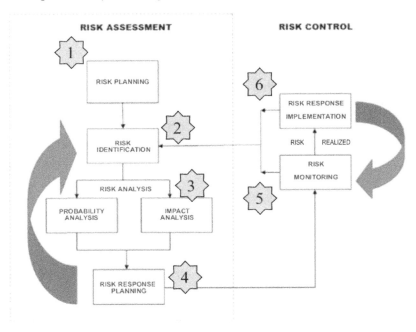

Figure 12: Framework Tailoring Decision Points

10

A MODEL RISK MANAGEMENT PLAN

Goals and Principles of Risk Management

The primary goal of risk management is to navigate the uncertainty found in any initiative. Actions may range from identifying ways to complete the initiative in a timelier, more cost-effective manner, or both to problems that may derail the initiative or cause total failure. In an ideal world, the benefits of opportunities would offset (or better) the impacts of issues.

As the development of the risk management plan and risk assessment workshop begins, here are some general principles to keep in mind to guide decision-making:

The organization and initiative stakeholders have attitudes toward risk. These attitudes will affect thinking throughout the process and need to be determined in advance. Use the Risk Assessment Workshop Risk Profile template as an information-gathering tool (see Appendix B). Consider other avenues of information gathering – please see the Risk Profile and Information Gathering tool descriptions in Section III for additional detail.

Risk assessment – identification, analysis, and response planning – is a team task. The best thinking comes from diversity, many ideas, and following a process. The initiative team and other key stakeholders need to work on the process collaboratively. The initiative manager may facilitate but cannot do the work alone.

It is impossible to identify all uncertainty. Therefore, the risk categories include "unknown unknowns". These are the unidentified opportunities and threats that may present themselves during the execution of the initiative. While not identifiable in advance, do record them as this may be helpful for future endeavors.

Focus on finding the highest priority risks. Since it is impossible to identify all uncertainty, try to focus on the highest priority risks – those with the highest impact and likelihood. To do so requires a breadth and depth of thinking, knowledge, and experience.

Timebox risk assessments. Because all uncertainty is not identifiable and the process needs to be scalable and proportionate to the initiative's size, allocate some fixed time. Somewhere between 1% and 10% of the overall initiative timeline is a good rule of thumb. Remember, assessments may need repetition from time-to-time, so do not expend all the allocated time on the initial evaluation.

No two risk assessments will produce the same result. Due to the human thinking involved, no two teams will come up with the same assessment. The same team will not have the same result on different days. Therefore, it is best to consider risk continuously. If risk tolerance is low, consider engaging more than one team in work or split the team. This will increase the diversity of thinking, avoid group-think, and improve the odds of identifying all significant risks.

Bias is inevitable. Psychologists have identified over 100 cognitive biases affecting human thinking, including individual risk appetites and thresholds. While there is no "cure", the best way to start mitigating this is with a) teamwork following the process and b) strong facilitation (Buss 2005, Wikipedia 2020). A good facilitator encourages everyone to speak.

Alignment is important. Align risk responses to response strategies (e.g., do not make a significant, expensive change in plans for an accepted risk) and align the initiative goals' responses.

The Lifecycle of Risks

Risks have lifecycles within and between initiatives, beginning with their identification. Recognizing these states is essential for identifying status within the risk management plan and risk log. Move risks that are duplicates of another or rejected as not applicable by the team to an archive, where they are available for future consideration.

When responding and monitoring begins, and the trigger event occurs, the opportunity's benefit or the threat's impact is realized (either all at once or over time). Close the risk once the benefit or impact is fully realized and all response actions have been implemented. In some rare error cases where the benefits and effects are not complete, re-open the risk in the "realized" state. At the end of the initiative lifecycle, remove the risk to an archive (e.g., retain the risk log) for future consideration by new initiatives. Archived risks may be useful for including in lessons-learned, checklists, other lists of risks, and movement to logs of similar initiatives.

Figure 13 provides a pictorial overview of the risk lifecycle.

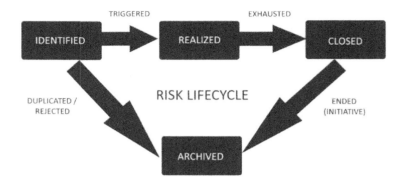

Figure 13: Risk Lifecycle

Risk Management Plan Contents

The risk management plan is a subset of the overall initiative plan (e.g., a project plan) which details strategies for navigating uncertainty throughout the initiative. The plan should clearly define all terms and spell out all aspects and decisions regarding the risk management process, including all selected and approved methods, tools, and techniques. The framework, this book, and the supplied template available should provide most of the material – as tailoring changes the framework, be sure to update the plan accordingly. A good plan should be highly re-usable for future initiatives.

For a complete risk management plan document, consider the following document sections (also in the risk management plan template) for a comprehensive plan:

- **Title, Date, Author** – identifies the document and who is responsible for it
- **Document Control Information** – identifies the updates to the document, including when it updated, by whom, and the updates made
- **Table of Contents** – where to find information in the document
- **Purpose of the Document** – brief statement of goals for the document
- **Attitudes Toward Risk** – a statement of organizational and initiative attitudes toward risk such as risk tolerance or risk appetite (the tools and templates for the risk assessment workshop in Section III include forms for collecting this information from key stakeholders)
- **Overall Approach to Risk Management** – a summary of the risk management approach, overall; should typically be a brief description of the framework
- **Risk Management Process Steps** – each step with detailed information and decisions
  - **Risk Assessment Workshop** – recommended implementation for risk assessment; overview of the workshop
    - **Risk Identification** – details of methods for identification
    - **Risk Analysis** – details of methods for analysis
    - **Risk Response Planning** – details of methods for response planning
  - **Risk Monitoring** -details of methods for monitoring the initiative environment
  - **Risk Response Implementation** – details of the implementation of responses (e.g., when, and how)
- **Risk Management Tools and Techniques** – details of tools and techniques; at a minimum, include the risk assessment

workshop (RAW), RAID Log, and brainstorming techniques for the RAW; include methods for risk tracking and reporting
- **Processes for Handling Escalations and Unidentified Risks** – define these processes, which will mainly be specific to the organization, the initiative, or both
- **Plan Approvals** – signatures of critical stakeholders to record buy-in
- **Glossary** – definitions of terms
- **Appendices** – copies of forms used and other supplemental information

Chapter Summary

- Goals and principles:
  - The organization and initiative stakeholders have attitudes toward risk.
  - Risk assessment – identification, analysis, and response planning – is a team task.
  - It is impossible to identify all uncertainty.
  - Focus on finding the highest priority risks.
  - Timebox risk assessments.
  - No two risk assessments will produce the same result.
  - Bias is inevitable.
  - Alignment is important.
- Risks have lifecycles
  - Identified
  - Realized
  - Closed
  - Archived
- A well-developed and written risk management plan can serve future initiatives.

CHAPTER 11

USING A FUNCTIONAL RISK REGISTER

Introduction to a Risk Log

A well-laid-out risk log, also known as a risk register, will serve as a repository for all necessary risk-related data for the initiative. It is created when planning for risk management and updated throughout the process. The data should, at a minimum, include:

- Identified opportunities and threats
- Analysis (relative probability and impacts) to provide prioritization
- Risk responses – actions taken to either alter plans or upon the occurrence of the risk trigger for those risks with the highest priorities
- Status of each risk and any in-progress responses

Initiative initiation may identify preliminary risks, so make at least a minimal log available by that time. The risk management planning process of the framework should include the details of the risk log. A completed log is an output of the last part of the risk assessment workshop, risk response planning. This log needs update during risk monitoring and risk response implementation, throughout the risk management process, and the initiative's life cycle.

If there are more than a few dozen risks, having a visual display is essential to understand the data better. Visuals should include a Risk Assessment Matrix to see opportunities and threats by priority, plus charts showing risks by category, response status, strategy, and other vital data.

A simplified risk log template containing fields for the minimum information accompanies this book. Its design enables the capture of minimum details with a focus on prioritization and simple actions. It is an excellent choice for those that want to try the framework "as is", with minimum tailoring. It places a burden on the initiative manager and team to understand the costs and time impacts of both risks and their responses.

A more advanced form of risk log is a Risks, Actions, Issues, and Decisions or RAID log. An interactive RAID log template, which will help many forms of initiatives, is available to readers of this book (see Appendix B for template information). It enables the collection and use of more advanced information, such as the cost and time impacts of the risks and responses. However, it too can capture the most basic information. While it is a little more overhead to learn to use, it contains a dashboard that automatically creates a risk assessment matrix and provides additional statistical information.

Understanding the RAID Log Template

The RAID log template provided with this book uses Microsoft Excel and is interactive. It works with virtually every Excel version; however, some of the Risks tab features require a Microsoft operating system. With minor accommodations, the RAID log is usable with Apple and other devices without Microsoft operating systems. Only a small portion of functionality is reliant on the Microsoft platform.

When opening the RAID log file, depending on the system and settings in use, it may be necessary to accept one or two warning messages. These may appear in different formats depending on the Excel version in use; however, they both serve the same purpose. The first message enables editing since the file may initially open in Protected View, commonly used by Microsoft Office products to warn of a file downloaded from the internet. Click the Enable Editing button to exit the Protected View and enter risk data:

Figure 14: Excel Enable Editing

Once editing is enabled, a second message may ask for permission to allow the active content: macros and Visual Basic code, which make the spreadsheet interactive:

99

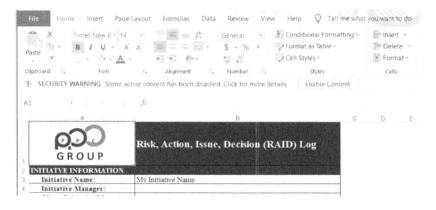

Figure 15: Excel Enable Content

Once selecting Enable Content, the workbook is ready to use.

The workbook consists of five tabs:

- Initiative Info – records information identifying the initiative, key stakeholders, and attitudes toward risk
- Risks – an interactive sheet to record information about the opportunities and threats
- Risk Dashboard – a series of visual displays populated by the Risks tab (locked to prevent edits)
- Actions & Decisions – a sheet to record critical steps and decisions taken and made during the risk management process
- (Lookups) – a sheet containing data to manage the drop-down lists and other interactive features (locked to prevent edits)

To record a risk, press the Add New Risk button at the top of the Risks sheet.   Note: if not using a Microsoft operating system, copy the first row of the sheet multiple times (once for each risk) starting

100

in row five, just below the risks table header. If the drop-down lists for the Category, Probability, Impact, Status, or Strategy columns are not functioning, type in the values in the same manner as they appear on the (Lookup) tab for those columns.

Drop-down lists support data entry for the Category, Probability, Impact, Status, or Strategy columns. If this functionality is not supported, type in the data as it appears on the (Lookup) tab. Proper entry updates the dashboard visuals. A complete list of all RAID log columns and their purpose appears in Appendix A: RAID Risk Tab Columns. In the event the Risk Dashboard tab is not displaying correct data, please check the content of the Category, Probability, Impact, Status, and Strategy columns.

Use the Actions & Decisions tab to record all assumptions, constraints, actions, and decisions which are not already on the Risks tab. As periodic reviews occur, be sure to consider and maintain this information.

Communicating Risks to Stakeholders

The RAID log contains everything needed to communicate effectively about risks to all stakeholders. The dashboard visuals can be beneficial for sharing with senior management:

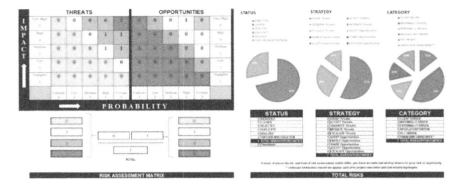

Figure 16: Risk Dashboard Example

Using the filtering and sorting features of the Risk sheet, it is possible to isolate the top 5-10 risks for any period to include in status reports and other management communications. The Risk sheet data contains the raw data the initiative manager and initiative team may need to stay informed about risks and navigate uncertainty.

The creation of a complete initiative communication plan is a best practice. Extend the RAID log template as necessary to provide all the data needed to fulfill the communication plan.

Documenting Risks for Future Initiatives

The data in the risk log at the end of the initiative includes valuable information and data for both the organization and future endeavors. As an initiative using the log ends:

- Conduct a lessons-learned session where a portion of the session focuses on the risk management process.

102

- Use lessons-learned to create a small change for continuous improvement using plan, do, check, act (PDCA), again specific to the risk management process.
- Review the risks in the risk log and determine which may apply to future initiatives.
- Add risks applicable to future initiatives to a checklist (best practice: include a new checklist tab in future risk logs).
- Assemble repeated responses into another checklist.
- Preserve the entire log in a read-only state to make data available for future initiatives (e.g., Estimated Monetary Value data associated with specific risk responses).

Experience has shown that anywhere from one to five years is a reasonable retention period for risk logs associated with past initiatives.

Chapter Summary

- A useful risk log contains all the risk-related data and makes it easy to access. Minimum data includes:
  - Identified opportunities and threats
  - Risk responses – actions taken to either alter plans or upon the occurrence of the risk trigger for those risks with the highest priorities
  - Status of each risk and any in-progress responses
  - Analysis (relative probability and impacts) to provide prioritization
- A RAID (risks, actions, issues, and decisions) can be useful for more involved initiatives or reporting risk data. A RAID log with a Risk Dashboard accompanies this book (see Appendix B).
- Save risk logs as historical information for future initiatives. Begin to look for everyday, universal risks for your organization and its initiatives.

CHAPTER 12

CONDUCTING A SUCCESSFUL RISK ASSESSMENT WORKSHOP (RAW)

Setting the Agenda

Risk assessment workshops can be transformative experiences, and like any other meeting, they require planning to be effective. Use the Risk Assessment Workshop Agenda Template, as appropriate (see Appendix B), to form and communicate the plan. Reflect any time boxing/scaling decisions about the risk assessment workshop in the final agenda.

Distribute the agenda at least three to five days in advance of the meeting so participants have adequate time to understand the initiative and formulate their questions and thoughts about it. Sessions may take a day or less for most small- to medium-sized initiatives. Alternatively, they may span several days for more complex and longer-term initiatives. Usually, no more than one to three days should be allocated. It would be sporadic that more than a week would be required. Gaps in the agenda will allow the team to address action items between meeting segments.

At a minimum, consider the following items for the agenda:

- Welcome message to participants
- Roles and responsibilities – who is facilitating, taking notes, and managing time?
- Overview of the risk management processes
- Time-boxed brainstorming sessions (including some alternative facilitation techniques) to consider:
  - Risk identification
  - Risk analysis (likelihood and impact, potentially separate meetings)
  - Risk ownership assignments (potentially determined between sessions)
  - Risk responses (e.g., strategy, actions, time, and dollar costs)
- A lessons-learned session to both collect team attitudes toward the process and determine improvement for the next workshop
- A closing session to summarize action items and results of the meetings

The agenda should include consideration of which brainstorming techniques to use for each session. In general, merely switching techniques will have benefits. In addition to traditional brainstorming, brainswarming, the Delphi method, and Six Thinking Hats will be useful techniques for identifying and possibly analyzing. In brief:

- Brainswarming uses drawing instead of speaking, allowing for faster idea generation.
- Delphi helps when there are strong technical opinions by gathering the ideas anonymously.
- Six Thinking Hats allows the examination of problems and data from multiple angles.

More details for each of these are in Section III.

It can be challenging to switch from identifying opportunities to identifying threats and vice versa. Once establishing a positive or negative "thinking" pattern, it is difficult to change the mindset. Some potential ways to address this are:

- Schedule separate sessions for opportunities and threats
- Identify opportunities first, within the same session
- Use separate teams to generate opportunities and threats (each reviews the work of the other)
- Use lateral thinking techniques such as Six Thinking Hats (experience has shown it is easy to teach and very effective at looking at circumstances in a variety of ways)
- Use Appreciative Inquiry for identification of opportunities

If there is an extensive core team participating in the brainstorming, consider Open Space, a form of multi-station brainstorming described in Chapter 14, Facilitated Meetings: Brainstorming.

Tip: When virtual teams over multiple time zones are involved, I have found the following information is essential to include directly in the agenda, especially if it is embedded within an electronic calendar/meeting invitation system, such as provided by Microsoft Outlook:

- List the names of all participants in the meeting within the embedded agenda. Some recipients will scan this list and compare it to the email list – you may find some omitted people or names misspelled. Do not trust that you will be informed of all misspelled names and undelivered mail.
- List date and time information, including time zone, along with how to enter the meeting by region or country. I have found that not all electronic systems these meeting invitations will pass through correctly interpret time zones,

leading to missed appointments. Use a service such as World Time Server (https://www.worldtimeserver.com/) to plan good meeting times and verify all time zone information.

Conducting the Workshop

All aspects of the workshop hinge on idea generation, collaboration, and the team's ability to think both broadly and deeply about the uncertainty the initiative will navigate. Isolate attendees from their day-to-day work for the best results. The meeting environment should be conducive to this work: comfortable seating and plenty of materials to capture outputs (e.g., whiteboards, markers, poster paper, etc.). Light refreshments should be continuously available and frequent short breaks between sessions to allow everyone to think time and work on action items.

The workshop needs the support of three roles held by a minimum of two people:

- **Facilitator**: Leads the sessions, encourages both broad and deep thinking on topics, and ensures everyone has a voice. The facilitator may form small groups to work collaboratively and then bring the team together to review results. Everyone needs to be engaged and active.
- **Scribe**: Documents the minutes of the meeting and organizes the brainstorming and other work outputs. Documents open issues and action items. Maintains a "parking lot" list for things to address later. Maintains the risk log and writes the final workshop report. Presented information must be bias-free and without

any "political spin". Due to the amount of documentation, the scribe role may require more than one person.

- **Time Keeper**: Keeps the meeting on track and assists the facilitator and scribe as necessary for the meeting's smooth flow and complete capture of information.

When assigning the roles to people, keep in mind that both the scribe and the facilitator play significant roles requiring constant attention. It would, therefore, be best if facilitation and scribing responsibilities were assigned to two different people.

When risk identification and analysis are complete, the facilitator needs to focus on the highest priority items. Commonly, so many risks emerge that it is virtually impossible to address them all. After a typical workshop, it would be expected for most "accepted" risks to have no further notes or actions associated with them.

Complete documentation ensures success. Maintain a parking lot list for items to address later in or outside of the workshop. Maintain work for between sessions or after the workshop on an action items list—record critical decisions and actions in the risk log.

Tip: Particularly complex, difficult, or sensitive projects or those where the project team has not demonstrated an ability to work well together may benefit from professional facilitation. Please visit the International Association of Facilitators website (IAF 2017).

Documenting the Workshop and Updating the Risk Log

If risk owners are responsible for determining post-workshop actions, do not consider the workshop complete until there is a separate meeting to review action plans. The meeting is essential to ensure the documentation is complete.

There are two primary outputs of the risk assessment workshop to document the results: the completed risk log and the Risk Assessment Workshop Report. Update any initiative budgets and timelines with contingency reserves (an amount set aside to cover identified risks) and management reserves (an amount set aside to cover unidentified risks). Reserves are exclusively for risks and should not cover change requests not connected to risks (please refer to chapters 4, 5, and 9 to understand contingency reserves better).

The completed RAID log should have all columns filled, except for the Date Finalized column. This last column only indicates risk closure. Closed means:

- The risk has become a benefit or an issue
- All planned actions are complete
- The risk has been successfully mitigated or avoided – no further benefits or issues relating to it are expected

The Risk Assessment Workshop Report is a document that summarizes the workshop results and the necessary steps for moving forward. The minimum sections of this report should include:

- **Title, Date, Author** – identifies the document and who is responsible for it
- **Document Control Information** – identifies the updates to the document, including when it updated, by whom, and a record of updated content
- **Table of Contents** – where to find information in the document
- **Executive Summary** – short summarization of the report, including:
  - Purpose of the Document (include background information about the initiative, stakeholders with interest in the document, and document recipients)
  - Related Documents (e.g., Risk Management Plan, Risk Log, memos, and agendas)
  - Overall Approach to the Risk Assessment Workshop
  - Summary of Results
- **Risk Assessment Workshop** – details of workshop sessions, highlighting highest priority risks
  - **Risk Identification** – details risk identification
  - **Risk Analysis** – details of risk analysis
  - **Risk Response Planning** – details of risk response planning
- **Action Items** – document any action items remaining after the workshop
- **Glossary** – definitions of terms (may copy from risk management plan document)
- **Appendices** – as needed to include supplemental information (e.g., meeting minutes)

As a result of the workshop analysis, Estimated Monetary Value (EMV) and Estimated Time Value (ETV) may be determined to record in the risk log. Section III documents how to estimate the impact of the risk in terms of dollars and time. These are negative values for opportunities (savings of dollars or time) and positive for threats (addition of dollars or time).

As a part of risk response planning, estimate the cost and time for implementing the response actions. Compare these to the EMV and ETV. Suppose the response consumes more cost and time to implement. In that case, it may be necessary to either find alternative responses or update the EMV and ETV to larger numbers. It is possible to sum the EMV and ETV columns individually to provide contingency reserve amounts in an ideal world. These amounts also guide management reserves' needs (please see chapters 4, 5, and 9, which define and elaborate more on contingency and management reserves).

Once the response plans are complete, it may become necessary to re-prioritize some risks, updating the likelihood and impact. For example, a project plan or work methods may need an update to avoid a risk that is both certain and very high impact. With the avoidance actions in place, the likelihood and impacts will most likely be lower. Update the documentation for these risks to reflect the correct priority.

Small-to-medium-sized initiatives and organizations may estimate the contingency reserve as a percentage of the overall budget and time, generally up to 10-15% of the budget or time. Constrain the use of the contingency reserve to the identified risks, as documented in the risk log. The initiative manager typically has the authority to spend the contingency reserve.

The estimation of management reserves for unidentified risks is more complicated. These may be amounts of between 5-10% of the overall budget and timeline. Constrain the expenditures of these amounts to risks with the category "Unknown Unknowns". Seek management permission before using these reserves.

It is not unusual for smaller initiatives to forego this analysis and add a 15-25% reserve to cover both contingency and management reserves. To avoid later surprises, the initiative manager must work diligently to compute EMV and ETV. These amounts may be far more or less than a fixed percentage.

When the risk log is as complete as possible, it helps sort the risks in priority order. The primary focus should always be on the top priority risks which have looming triggers within the review period. The lower priority accepted risks need less frequent review

Tip: For new or accidental project managers or any other initiative manager trying the risk assessment framework for the first time, it should be adequate to compute the relative likelihood and impact and assign a fixed percentage to the budget and time allocations. Larger, more complex initiatives occurring later in careers may require more complex analytical techniques.

Chapter Summary

- A well-conducted risk assessment workshop (RAW) has a good plan and agenda.
- Three essential workshop roles are:
  - o Facilitator: guides the meeting
  - o Scribe: documents the result
  - o Timekeeper: keeps the meeting on track
- Document the results in a report and the risk log.

SECTION III: TOOLS AND TECHNIQUES SUPPORTING THE RISK ASSESSMENT FRAMEWORK

"If it's a good idea, go ahead and do it. It's much easier to apologize than it is to get permission."

— Rear Admiral Grace Hopper

CHAPTER 13

RISK PLANNING TOOLS AND TECHNIQUES

Information Gathering Techniques

Good information gathering is essential for all aspects of risk management, starting with planning and continuing throughout each step of the process. Some of the fundamental techniques include:

- **Surveys, questionnaires, and Interviews**: Distribute to critical stakeholders and subject matter experts to collect information. Distribute survey results to share the knowledge and follow up with one-on-one interviews for questionnaires to confirm results. Surveys, questionnaires, and interviews are an excellent way to make initial contact and introduce information about the initiative and risk management.
- **Observation**: Observe people and processes at work. Observation may be passive (no interaction with those performing the tasks) or active (doing the work side-by-side with participants, asking questions, and confirming observations as necessary).

- **Document Review**: Reviewing key organization and initiative documents, particularly governing documents such as policies and procedures. These may provide insights into risk attitudes to include in the risk profiles.
- **Facilitated Meetings**: Facilitated meetings using various brainstorming forms will form the basis for risk identification, analysis, and response planning as part of the risk assessment workshop.

It is essential to employ multiple information gathering methods to ensure a complete gathering and confirmation of information.

Risk Profile: Risk Appetite, Tolerance, and Threshold

A good risk profile will provide a snapshot of organizational and initiative stakeholder attitudes toward risk. In initiative management, this is analogous to the way a financial advisor may determine investment attitudes. It is vital to create a profile as the attitudes uncovered will constrain and even bias thinking going forward.

Some important points to consider are:

- **Risk Appetite:** This is a measure of the amount of risk an organization or initiative stakeholders are willing to undertake to achieve their strategic goals. The appetite between these two groups may often differ. For example, an organization that desires to achieve high quality and reliability may have a minimal appetite for risk to achieve the goals. On the other hand, an R&D project within the organization may absorb more risk to achieve innovation.

- **Risk Tolerance:** Risk tolerance measures the amount of variance from risk appetite the organization and initiative stakeholders are willing to accept. As pointed out by the previous example, this may differ depending on circumstances.
- **Risk Threshold:** This is the amount of risk that an organization or initiative stakeholders are willing to accept. For example, an organization may empower employees to make individual purchases of up to $1,000 for reimbursement and without management review.
- **Initial Risks:** Initiative stakeholders and subject matter experts may have some initial thoughts on the initiative's risks. Collect, consider, and add these as starter items to the risk log.

Various information gathering techniques will be necessary to complete this documentation. Document review will typically uncover overall organizational risk appetite, tolerance, and thresholds. Questionnaires and interviews will be essential to collect information for individual initiative stakeholders.

Tip: This is a great way to increase stakeholder engagement, even if they do not participate in the Risk Assessment Workshop.

Use the Risk Assessment Workshop Risk Profile template as an information-gathering tool (see Appendix B).

SWOT Analysis

In general, a SWOT (strength, weaknesses, opportunities, and threats) analysis may occur before starting an initiative. If this is the case, the initiative manager should obtain a copy and incorporate it into the documentation. If not, a SWOT analysis may assist in the high-level identification of opportunities and threats.

The acronym, SWOT, guides the identification process:

- **S**trengths: what are the strengths and competitive advantages of the business or initiative?
- **W**eaknesses: what would place the business or initiative at a disadvantage?
- **O**pportunities: what are the things outside of the business or initiative to exploit for the initiative's advantage?
- **T**hreats: what are the difficulties or roadblocks the initiative may face?

List these elements in a four-quadrant chart. There are several ways to use the data. For example, consider matching strengths with the best opportunities that play to those strengths. Take steps to improve on weaknesses or proactively address threats to build future strengths and opportunities. Threats and weaknesses may translate to risks to incorporate into threat identification (Gomer and Hille 2015). Similarly, strengths and opportunities may be initiative opportunities.

Tip: A SWOT analysis by itself may not be useful, but it can become a powerful tool when combined with strategic planning, corporate planning, business analysis activities, or initiative opportunity and threat analysis.

Model Risk Management Plan, RAID Log, and Risk Assessment Workshop

To provide the best support for the implementation of the risk assessment framework and the risk assessment workshop, use the templates and tools which accompany this book:

- Risk Assessment Framework Implementation Checklist
- Risk Management Plan template
- Risk Assessment Workshop Profile template
- Risk Assessment Workshop Agenda template
- Risk Assessment Workshop Process Overview presentation template
- Risk Assessment Workshop Report template
- Risk logs:
  - Simplified risk log for those just starting (with a training presentation)
  - RAID (risks, actions, issues, and decisions) log template requiring little or no modification and with a pre-filled example
- For instructors using this book:
  - A set of three slide lectures covering the materials
  - A potential team assignment using the RAID log
  - A three-level outline of the second edition book
- Access to all the first edition tools and templates, including:
  - A short Six Thinking Hats presentation
  - Mind map supporting the first edition

Please refer to Appendix B for details on how to access and modify all of these.

Chapter Summary

Risk planning tools and techniques include:

- Information gathering techniques
- Risk profile
- SWOT analysis
- Tools, techniques, and templates included with this book

CHAPTER 14

RISK IDENTIFICATION TOOLS AND TECHNIQUES

Categories

Having several categories available to divide up risks is an aid to obtaining the completeness of identification. The Sources of Risk: A Taxonomy chart provides a means for attendees at facilitated meetings to group risks into more categories than the traditional known knowns, known unknowns, and unknown unknowns. Supplement the categories with a list of universal risks and risks specific to the industry, company, or initiative. Group these specific risks using different categories as appropriate.

Tip: As part of early planning, develop the categories to keep everyone on the same page as the risk assessment workshop begins.

The chart is available in Figure 17; a PowerPoint version of the graphic is also available (see Appendix B).

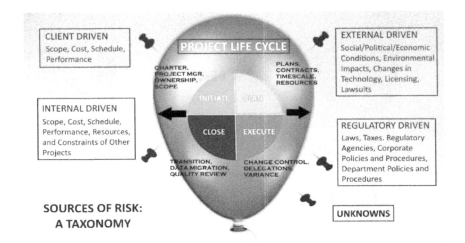

Figure 17: Sources of Risk: A Taxonomy

Other lists of categories from acronyms often used in business, especially in strategic planning, are possible. These include:

- **PESTLE** – Political, Economic, Social, Technological, Legal, Environmental
- **STEEPLE** – Social, Technological, Economic, Environmental, Legal, Ethical
- **VUCA** – Volatility, Uncertainty, Complexity, Ambiguity
- **TECOP** – Technological, Environmental, Commercial, Operational, Political
- **SPECTRUM** – Socio-cultural, Political, Economic, Competitive, Technological, Regulatory, Uncertainty, Market

Checklists

Take the right steps in the correct sequence by using checklists. A typical example of this is the checklist pilots go through before a takeoff. Another example is the company property return checklist when an individual exits an employment or volunteer situation. As experience with risk management in organizations grows, develop lists of common opportunities, threats, or issues to ensure future consideration.

The right level of detail in a checklist ensures the organization does not see them as bureaucratic. Adding a place to sign initials for completed items or a management sign-off to a list emphasizes the importance of the list elements and of following the process represented by the list.

Facilitated Meetings

Brainstorming

A facilitated meeting is a standard method to reach a consensus or decide. Simple brainstorming is an example of a facilitated session. Risk identification is a particular case, as there are many items in need of identification, analysis, and discussion. The facilitator of the meeting needs to maintain an environment conducive to completing the tasks at hand. Creating the environment includes setting basic ground rules for behavior and participation in the discussion, including:

- Maintain an atmosphere of mutual respect
- Build on ideas and be receptive to new ones

- Encourage and allow everyone to speak
- Prevent the business or topic owner from being the dominant voice
- Keep on task
- Determine how to handle unresolved issues

Brainstorming as a facilitated meeting is not always effective because it relies on a discussion. Experts may dominate or intimidate other participants. Open Space, a form of multi-station brainstorming, helps overcome this issue by engaging participants in multiple, simultaneous brainstorming sessions.

Tip: Another weakness with traditional brainstorming is the team may get "stuck in a rut." They may identify long lists of similar risks that could more effectively be treated as one. For example, the team may identify accidents, engine problems, brake failure, and running out of gas as possible risks for transportation. But merely placing a car breakdown as the threat may suffice. Be sure the facilitator recognizes when the team gets into this state and re-directs them to more productive areas.

There are four facilitated-meeting approaches, outside of simple brainstorming, which have some strength in dealing with specific situations and overcoming brainstorming's weaknesses. These are the Delphi Technique, Six Thinking Hats, Brainswarming, and Appreciative Inquiry. We will define these here and provide references and additional tools.

Delphi Method

Widely dispersed experts may be difficult to gather in one place. Some experts may also be dominating; once they have voiced their opinions, others will not want to speak. The Delphi Method, developed by the Rand Corporation in the 1950s, is an excellent way to handle these circumstances (RAND 2019).

The Delphi facilitator develops documents and questionnaires stating the problems to be solved, the inputs required, and the opinions needed. For example: "What do you think the greatest risks are for Project X?" Participants judge answers on a scale of one to ten or a similar objective scheme.

Questionnaires are collected, and the results are analyzed statistically and summarized. The results are sent with additional questions that may probe further into areas identified as key. The inputs from subsequent rounds may include ranking ideas and further clarifications of questions. This process continues until a consensus emerges; there are usually four or more rounds, potentially involving up to 50 experts. A significant drawback is the required time. Months or even a year might not be out of the question for a long-term project.

Six Thinking Hats

Six Thinking Hats is a technique created by Dr. Edward de Bono, who is best known for originating "lateral thinking" (or structured creativity). Six Thinking Hats enhances group thinking by helping teams break out of the habitual thinking processes and make better decisions. There is a better understanding of the decision's complexity, and new opportunities and issues may surface.

Through Six Thinking Hats, the team can better estimate the resistance to change, make creative leaps, and develop more thoughtful and complete contingency plans. Six Thinking Hats may be deployed for the entire risk assessment workshop or focus only on the contingency-planning steps. The facilitator of the risk assessment workshop must determine the optimal approach for organizational and team circumstances.

In this technique, six colored hats represent roles team members must play. Depending on team size, some team members may need to wear multiple hats. The roles of the hats are:

- Blue Hat
    - Process control or meeting chair
    - Directs the wearing of hats (e.g., the green hat when ideas run dry, the black hat for contingency planning)
- Black Hat
    - Looks at things pessimistically and cautiously; sees why ideas will not work
    - Spots fatal flaws, weak points and prepares contingency plans
- White Hat
    - Focuses on data and facts; looks for gaps in knowledge
    - Analyzes and extrapolates from historical data
- Yellow Hat
    - Takes a positive and optimistic stance
    - Sees the benefits and value of the decision, plus the opportunities created
- Green Hat
    - Identifies creative solutions and opportunities
    - Engages in freewheeling thinking
- Red Hat
    - Engages in motional thinking
    - Uses intuition and gut reaction

The black hat's pessimistic view and the knowledge gaps sought by the white hat are excellent for generating mitigation plans and seeing potential issues in planned risk responses. The other hats make sure the team looks at the positive aspects of a solution: the red hat helps draw out intuition and emotional issues. The green hat makes sure the team creatively examines all possible solutions in a brainstorming mode. The green hat is most likely to identify opportunities.

There are various ways to determine how to wear the hats—attending a de Bono seminar is necessary to learn which methods work best. For now, let us assume the process hat will make the call as required.

The supporting tools for the risk assessment framework include a brief PowerPoint presentation on Six Thinking Hats that may introduce it to the risk assessment workshop team (De Bono 2000).

Brainswarming

Brainswarming is another facilitation technique with a focus on improving how to think about problems. Some experts recommend doing "swarming" with a comfortable group working together and is prepared ahead on what issues are to be solved.

Brainswarming improves on brainstorming by a shift from talking to drawing. Drawing allows for faster idea generation and review. Brainswarming requires a room with a lot of open space and surface(s) for illustration. The facilitator will encourage everyone to chart, draw, annotate drawings, and otherwise get out their ideas in a pictorial form.

The facilitator starts the brainswarm by drawing a series of rough pictures. This may begin with a view of who and what money is involved and a timeline or flow chart. Rough charts and graphics define the solution. It is possible to evaluate hundreds of solutions and either discard or investigate them within a short period.

The Harvard Business Review video (McCaffrey 2014) contains a great illustration. A power company wanted to solve a long-standing problem of de-icing power lines in the winter. As the pictures of solutions for the situation began to emerge, so did an unexpected answer: use the downdraft created by a helicopter.

One advantage of brainswarming is people can work both independently and together on ideas. Top-down thinkers may be better at putting together a big picture, while bottom-up thinkers can focus on details. Good brainswarming sessions allow these groups to connect and find solutions to difficult problems in a fraction of the time. Everyone gets to work in a way that plays to each's strengths and abilities to contribute to a solution, making brainswarming an excellent tool for team building as well (McCaffrey 2014).

Tip: IdeaPaint is a treatment that can turn any wall into an erasable whiteboard. Great for brainswarming as well as other facilitated techniques. Find out more at https://ideapaint.com/.

Appreciative Inquiry

Appreciative Inquiry (AI) is an excellent tool for the identification of opportunities. AI is not just a way to identify opportunities--it is a way of embracing them and achieving change. First, the team gathers, brainstorms the possibilities, and then collects additional information on the quality, significance, and magnitude of the opportunities' strengths.

At the start of an AI session, there are four key questions to explore:

- What has been a "best experience"?

- What do you value about your work, yourself, and the organization?
- What are the organization's core values (usually obtainable from strategic plans or other corporate documents)?
- If you had three wishes for the organization, what would they be?

AI is successful because:

- It does not focus on changing people, only the organization and its processes. Energy is high because they focus on what is good; there is a relief that the session is not about mistakes.
- It invites people to engage in describing the kinds of settings they desire for their work.
- It helps everyone see the need for change, explore new possibilities, and contribute to solutions.
- There is not a blank canvas - AI builds on the existing accomplishments. A new organization capitalizes on prior good work.
- Through the alignment of structures with purpose and principles, shared vision and beliefs translate into reality and revised practices.

Tip: For more information about designing and conducting Appreciative Inquiry, please visit The Appreciative Inquiry Commons (Champlain College 2017).

Risk Breakdown Structure

A risk breakdown structure (RBS) is a hierarchical visualization of risks organized by category. Introduce an RBS during the initial risk assessment workshop for large, complex initiatives. Smaller initiatives may use an RBS for subsequent identification sessions (remember, the framework's risk assessment portion is both iterative and recursive). Having the information grouped in this manner may aid in further thinking and identification. Figure 18 illustrates the RBS for the RAID log pre-filled example.

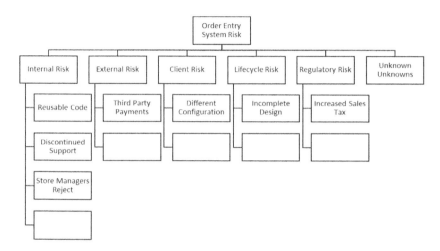

Figure 18: RBS Sample

Ishikawa Diagrams (Cause and Effect Analysis)

Cause-and-effect analysis, like force-field analysis, has its roots in problem-solving and decision-making. It is often a part of quality. Cause-and-effect analysis can also be useful in appropriate identification and analysis of risks, as well as in risk response planning.

One powerful cause-and-effect analysis tool is the Ishikawa or Fishbone Diagram, developed by Kaoru Ishikawa in 1968 (ASQ 2021). It is a specialized form of a mind map. Suppose a goal is to ensure a newly developed automobile has good gas mileage. State the problem on the left (the head of the fish) and draw a line as the spine.

As the next step, draw the prominent bones as diagonal lines. These are categories that group similar causes. Categories are not fixed—so, for example, consider people, methods, materials, and equipment. Smaller bones then represent causes and sub causes in their categories. A completed diagram of the problem might look like the one in this figure:

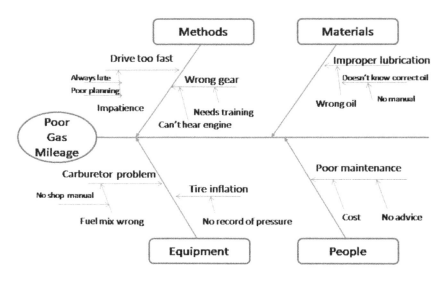

Figure 19: Fishbone Diagram Sample

The more detailed and complete the analysis, the more successful the outcomes will be. Based on the diagram, one might conclude to maximize consumer experience with gas mileage, risks of improper lubrication, improper maintenance, and incorrect fuel mixing need mitigation. Production of a shop and owner's manual containing the necessary information and advice may help consumers avoid these risks. A training course for mechanics may supplement the material If the new car is a radical departure from the past.

The Ishikawa diagram, like force-field analysis and other cause-and-effect methods, is not repeatable. Therefore, it is essential to be thorough and have a strong team working with the technique (MindTools 2017).

Force Field Analysis

Force-field analysis is a decision-making technique developed by Kurt Lewin in the 1940s. While initially intended for making decisions regarding changes, the application of force-field analysis to risk responses, such as changes to plans, is not very different.

Whiteboards typically record information for force field analysis, with the problem, proposed change, or response strategy in the middle. On the left, list the things that are for the change. On the right, list the things that are forces working against a change. Identify as many items on each list as possible, provide good facilitation, and include the right stakeholders in the analysis. Consider the following questions for the listed items:

- What are the business benefits of the change?
- Who are the stakeholders for and against the change?
- How easy is the change? What are the necessary costs, resources, and times to implement the change?
- What else does the change impact?
- In making the change, what new risks may emerge?

Completing the lists assigns a numerical score for each force, with one as a weak force and five as a potent force.

As an example, suppose an initiative is considering the automation of factory production. Here's how the analysis might look:

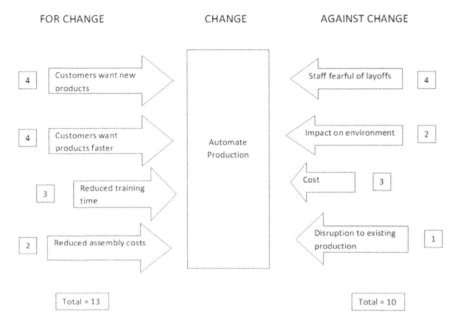

Figure 20: Force Field Diagram Sample

A completed force-field analysis may enable an immediate decision. However, it is more likely the findings will be used to refine the change to increase the forces on the left and decrease the forces on the right. For example, a human resources plan may determine the career path for those displaced by automation. The plan may divert resources to maintenance roles, involve monitoring the automated production and roles that include managing the conversion project (MindTools 2017).

Chapter Summary

Risk identification tools and techniques include:

- Categories
- Checklists
- Facilitated meetings
  - Brainstorming
  - Delphi Method
  - Six Thinking Hats
  - Brainswarming
  - Appreciative Inquiry
- Risk Breakdown Structure (RBS)
- Ishikawa Diagrams (Cause and Effect Analysis)
- Force Field Analysis

15

QUALITATIVE RISK ANALYSIS TOOLS AND TECHNIQUES

Risk Assessment Matrix (RAM, aka Probability-Impact Matrix)

The risk assessment matrix (RAM), also known as a probability-impact matrix (PIM), is an excellent way to visualize risk analysis results. It displays the combined effect of both impact and likelihood and helps guide risk response planning. The matrix consists of axes of impact and probability, usually divided into increasing scales of three, five, or ten items. Each cell records the number of risks with the given likelihood and impact. In this example, there are two, certain- probability, show-stopping threats, and one near-critical opportunity, which need action:

I M P A C T		Unlikely 1	Low 2	Medium 3	High 4	Certain 5	Unlikely 1	Low 2	Medium 3	High 4	Certain 5	
		THREATS					**OPPORTUNITIES**					
	Very High 5	0	0	0	0	2	0	0	0	1	0	Very High 5
	High 4	0	0	0	1	1	0	0	0	0	0	High 4
	Medium 3	0	0	0	1	1	0	0	0	0	0	Medium 3
	Low 2	0	0	0	0	0	0	0	0	0	0	Low 2
	Negligible 1	0	0	0	0	0	0	0	0	0	0	Negligible 1

PROBABILITY

Figure 21: Sample Risk Assessment Matrix

Associating a number with each point on the axis provides a way to see the interaction between likelihood and impact. The number is the multiplication of probability and impact. For example, a threat in the upper right-hand red box or an opportunity in the upper right-hand green box is five times five or twenty-five. Typically, any risk with a value of fifteen or greater needs the most and earliest attention. Note this type of arrangement also reinforces the strategy of starting mitigation activities in the upper right-hand corner and moving diagonally to the lower left-hand corner. This approach ensures attention focuses on the most critical risks.

Tip: One issue with the usual RAM is it only has twenty-five "buckets." While this will adequately prioritize hundreds of risks, thousands may be challenging to prioritize effectively. Of course, it is possible to extend the one-to-five scale to a one-to-ten scale, but that would not add much value. We recommend changing the scale to include zero at the low end and ninety-nine at the high end (just zero *and* ninety-nine, not all the numbers in between). Zero represents "no chance" and "no impact", while ninety-nine represents "absolute certainty" and "devastating consequences."

This approach adds a little more value in that it will both create more buckets and better isolate outliers. Let us look at possible value outcomes for this new scale:

Probability	Impact	Description
99	99	With the highest impact and likelihood, these events would be both certain and devastating (threats) or providing the highest benefit (opportunity) to the project. These are the risks that require the most attention on response plans.
99	n, n not 99	With the highest likelihood, these events are certain. Still, their impact will vary, and there will be a finer prioritization of these high-likelihood events. Also, record them as assumptions.
n, n not 99	99	These would be the most devastating (threats) or beneficial (opportunities) for the project with the highest impact. The likelihood will vary and provide a finer prioritization of these high-impact events, which require a good response plan.
0	0	These events are not a worry now but are on the list for potential change at the next risk assessment.

Table 2: Potential Extensions to Probability and Impact Scale

Even with smaller projects, this ranking is an excellent way to make the highest- (and lowest-) probability and impact risks stand apart from the others.

Failure Mode and Effects Analysis (FMEA)

Quality engineers developed failure Mode and Effects Analysis (FMEA) to study risks in production and manufacturing processes. FMEA analysis starts much like a formal risk analysis by determining each potential risk's impact and likelihood. FMEA typically uses a ten-point scale for this, with a one being low and a ten high. The detectability of the risk is the third factor. For example, a risk that is almost undoubtedly detectable by systems is assigned a one.

In contrast, a risk difficult or impossible to detect is assigned a ten. Calculate a risk priority number (RPN) by multiplying the likelihood, impact, and detectability together. The RPN can enter the risk management process as the priority, and risk response planning can occur (Tague 2005).

It is possible to modify the RAID log to support FMEA. The most straightforward approach might be to perform a separate analysis and record the RPN number in the log. There are hidden columns between "Impact" and "Severity" to unhide for that purpose. Modifying the drop downs and adding detectability and a calculated RPN column is also possible. A simplified FMEA analysis chart might appear as in figure 22:

FAILURE MODE AND EFFECTS ANAYSIS

Process Name: Fence Installation - Post Hole Drilling
Process ID:
Date:
Revision:
Team:

Failure Mode	A. Impact (1-10; 10 = Highest}	B. Probability (1-10; 10 = Highest)	C. Detectability (1-10; 10 = Lowest)	RPN A*B*C
Hole too deep	3	5	1	15
Hole not deep enough	2	5	2	20
Hit rock while drilling	10	3	8	240

Figure 22: FMEA Sample

Due to its similarity to FMEA in using additional factors to determine the risk priority, the quadratic formula may also be applied to remove more subjectivity in determining the risk rating.

Risk Data Quality Assessment

A risk data quality assessment is a means to determine the quality of data created for risk management, including the identification, prioritization, and impact analysis (PMI 2017). Assess in a manner like any other data quality assessment. The analytical step draws to a close, ensuring that the best possible information will inform the response strategies and actual responses.

An excellent risk data quality assessment examines the collected risk management data in a variety of dimensions, such as:

- Accessibility – is the data well organized and accessible

- Consistency – is all the data in the right format and internally consistent (e.g., are there similar risks that may have very different priorities)
- Credibility – is the data complete and believable
- Relevance – is all the data related and applicable to the initiative
- Unbiased – is the data free of bias and supported by facts and observable circumstances
- Validity – is the data of the right type and correct

After risk response planning, address data validity to ensure any changes indicated by the process are of good quality. An important point to check is consistency – the response strategies and actions should be in alignment/agreement with each other and with the selected priorities.

The accompanying RAID log design supports accessibility and consistency, and to some degree, validity. Drop-down lists are available where possible, along with the organization and guidance provided on how to enter the data.

Quadratic Six-Dimension Mean

One of the drawbacks of the usual probability-and-impact analysis is it can be subjective and error-prone for many reasons, including:

- Lack of objective data
- Thinking traps (also known as cognitive biases) and judgment errors
- Incorrect thinking about and treatment of sunk costs
- Other planning errors entering the process

How some people view air travel is an example of bias. Because a plane crash is usually a fiery and devastating event, some tend to think of air travel as risky and even unsafe. However, when looking at objective data, such as the ratio of deaths per thousand passengers, air travel is relatively safe than other transportation modes. In fact, in the US, passenger deaths by driving are 750 times higher per mile than for flying (Wikipedia 2021).

Adopting the Quadratic Mean Process to Quantify the Qualitative Risk Analysis (Vargas) suggests capturing relative impact in six dimensions, including:

- Time
- Cost
- Quality
- Safety and security
- Other
- Proximity (the time horizon to a risk event)

The impact is the quadratic mean (root square mean) of these dimensions.

Tip: A paper with formula details (Vargas 2013) is available as a free download for PMI members: http://marketplace.pmi.org/Pages/ProductDetail.aspx?GMProduct=00101518300 (there is a fifteen-dollar charge for non-members).

Monte Carlo Simulation

Monte Carlo simulations can evaluate overall project risks and outcomes, plus assess cost and schedule risks and impacts. Monte Carlo simulations are computer programs that can quickly run through thousands of iterations and scenarios to develop project outcome predictions based on probabilities and statistics.

The technique is beneficial for analyzing large projects, their critical paths, and their near-critical paths. Recall the critical path is the shortest path to project completion, and each task on the critical path has no slack. As a result, critical-path tasks must complete on time to keep the project on track. A Monte Carlo simulation can help evaluate the critical path and the effects project changes may have on it.

Monte Carlo simulation and schedule-review tools are available as add-ons to Microsoft Project.

Chapter Summary

Qualitative analysis tools and techniques include:

- Risk Assessment Matrix (RAM)
- Failure Mode and Effects Analysis (FMEA)
- Risk Data Quality Assessment
- Quadratic Six-Dimension Mean
- Monte Carlo Simulation

CHAPTER 16

QUANTITATIVE ANALYSIS TOOLS AND TECHNIQUES

Expected Monetary and Time Value

Estimate the financial and time impact of a risk, then compute the estimated monetary value (EMV) and estimated time value (ETV). They are simply the product of the likelihood and the impact (dollars or time). These values will both help to inform the contingency reserves and expenditure on risk response.

Note while the EMV has fixed units (dollars or other local currency), the ETV should have a measure assigned that is relevant to the initiative and then maintained for consistency. For example, a short timeline with relatively small risk impacts might choose days. A longer, multi-year initiative might choose weeks or months. Regardless of choice, consistent use allows for a quick sum of the totals for all or groups of risks.

When using the risk assessment framework and the supplied RAID log, there are three immediately possible approaches:

1. **Detailed probability and impact**. If the chance is determined to be 63% (or 0.63) and the actual time impact is determined to be ten days, the ETV is 0.63 x 10 = 6.3 days.
2. **Relative probability and detailed impact**. Given that probabilities are often more difficult to estimate with any accuracy, assign each of the RAID log values to a relative probability (Certain = 100%, High = 80%, Medium = 60%, Low = 40%, Unlikely = 20%). If the probability is determined to be medium and the cost impact is $1,000, then the EMV is 0.60 x 1,000 = $600.
3. **Relative probability and relative impact**. For this approach, use the probabilities as defined above. Develop a set of relative dollars and times for impacts that are appropriate for the initiative. For example, Very High = 20 days, High = 15 days, Medium = 10 days, Low = 5 days, and Negligible = 2 days. If the probability is high and the time impact medium, the ETV is 0.80 x 10 = 8 days.

For new and accidental project managers, the latter two approaches are likely adequate. The EMV and ETV estimates are sufficiently accurate for most initiative needs. As initiatives become more complex, more skilled initiative managers will need to move toward the first approach.

Decision Trees

Like the analysis of a chess game, a decision tree first involves constructing all possible paths and decisions. Each decision branch has a potential route and records the likelihood and impact of taking each specific route. Summing together all the components of the decision tree determines the best course of action. Decision trees are versatile tools for diverse applications, such as optimizing a portfolio or choosing a product to develop. In risk, decision trees aid the analysis of more complex decisions and outcomes, along with response plans.

They are usually straightforward to create, understand, and explain to others. Even without exact numbers to fill in, mapping out the choices is insightful.

Consider the following simple decision tree deciding if a production line should be automated. If automation is not implemented, nothing is risked or lost. If there is a low demand for the product (estimated to be 50%), $90,000 is lost if automation is implemented. Since the chances of medium or high demand are low, the risk of automating the line may be avoided until there is more experience with the product's demand. If demand increases, it may be time to revisit this decision tree to see if it is still valid.

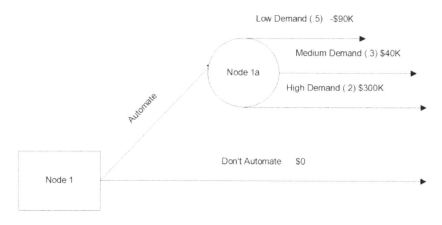

Figure 23: Decision Tree Sample

PERT Estimation

Booz Allen Hamilton developed the Program Evaluation and Review Technique (PERT) in 1957 to manage the risk of more than 10,000 contractors on the Polaris missile project (Kletter 2019). The emphasis of PERT is to control the schedule with flexible costs. PERT's fundamental basis is developing a weighted average using the most likely, an optimistic, and a pessimistic estimate.

Hopefully, PERT estimation is already in use for initiative timelines. If it is not, a good starting point would be for improved estimates of risk impacts if getting an accurate estimate is essential. The advantages of using PERT are:

- The range of the estimate is computed, not guessed
- The initiative manager, to a degree, can choose the range accuracy
- The odds of reaching a specific client end date are computable
- When a client wants a probability of success, the date range meeting can be determined

To start, develop three estimates: the pessimistic time (P), the optimistic time (O), and the most likely time (M) for each risk impact. Remember that for opportunities, these should be negative, and for threats, positive. The basic PERT formula for a risk impact is:

$$\frac{P + 4M + O}{6} \pm \sqrt{\left(\frac{P - O}{6}\right)^2}$$

Equation 2: PERT Estimation Formula

where

$$\left(\frac{P - O}{6}\right)^2$$

Equation 3: PERT Variance Formula

is the variance (variance measures the volatility of the estimate's mean).

The confidence level of this estimate is one standard deviation of approximately 68%. Doubling the range represents the confidence level at two standard deviations of about 95%. This level of accuracy is adequate for nearly all initiatives.

To provide a complete example, consider a threat estimated with a pessimistic impact of 20 days, an optimistic impact of 10 days, and a most likely impact of 12 days.

The estimated impact for the risks is then:

$$= \frac{20 + (4 \times 12) + 10}{6} \pm \sqrt{\left(\frac{P - O}{6}\right)^2}$$

$$= \frac{78}{6} \pm \sqrt{4}$$

$$= 13 \pm 2 \text{ days with 68\% confidence}$$

$$= 13 \pm 4 \text{ days with 95\% confidence}$$

Rather than provide a mathematics lesson, it is possible to determine the chances of success for a given number of days or a probability using Excel formulas. If

- z = Probability of completion at the desired time
- D = Desired completion time, say 15 days
- μ = PERT computed completion time
- $v = \sqrt{\left(\frac{P-O}{6}\right)^2}$

then, using Excel formula z=NORM.DIST(D, μ, v, TRUE) and plugging in the variables, NORM.DIST(15, 13, 2, TRUE) is 0.84. In other words, we have an 84% chance of meeting the schedule within 15 days. Note that our PERT estimate has a 50% chance of success using the normal distribution curve.

Similarly, the Excel formula D=NORM.INV(z, μ, v) provides the number of days necessary to meet a probability of z. If 75% confidence is a requirement, then NORM.INV(.75, 13, 2) indicates we can address the time impact in about 14 days with 75% confidence (Meredith, Shafer, & Mantel 2014).

Tip: While PERT supports time estimation, it can also make a promising approach for estimating complex budgets. I have often used it for both.

Risk-Benefit Analysis

A risk-benefit analysis, conducted similarly to a cost-benefit analysis, evaluates the risk and considers its benefits. As an example, as individuals, we accept a certain amount of personal risk every day. Getting in a car exposes us to risks such as accidents. Still, the benefit is saving time and money by moving around more effectively.

Determining the totals of costs and benefits requires detailed analysis to ensure all major costs and benefits are included. Let us say, for example, a team is evaluating the risk of replacing a paper-based system with an imaging solution. Examples of the existing paper-based system's costs might include paper, file folders, cabinets, storage space, and personnel time to manage paper and storage, copy machines, and so on. The scanning solution would involve the costs of scanners and computers, storage media, housing for computer equipment, personnel to operate equipment, and so on. Take enough time to estimate and analyze potential costs.

Divide benefits into two categories—hard dollar benefits and "soft," non-financial benefits. A hard dollar benefit of the scanning solution might be personnel costs saved in looking for lost documents. The saved costs might also be an opportunity. A soft benefit might be the more modern and up-to-date appearance for potential customers who visit the facilities.

Tip: Looking at the ratio of costs and benefits alone is usually not enough since two risks may have the same ratio but differ in costs to mitigate by millions. Therefore, it is crucial to make sure the selected responses will fit budgets or come with opportunities to offset them. It is also important to be very careful to include all the major costs and benefits. Having a third party examine the analysis to ensure an independent review may be helpful.

Chapter Summary

Quantitative risk management tools and techniques include:

- Expected Monetary Value (EMV), Expected Time Value (ETV)
- Decision Trees
- PERT Estimation
- Risk-Benefit Analysis

CHAPTER **17**

RISK RESPONSE PLANNING TOOLS AND TECHNIQUES

A Process for Risk Response Planning

Developing a process for risk response planning is critical. A process reduces thinking bias, the risk of inadequate responses. It ensures that any newly created risks receive treatment as all others.

Risk response planning is both an iterative (repeated) and a recursive (need to return to previous steps) process. Examine each risk in the risk log in priority order. This process will iterate until either all risks have responses or all the highest priority risks have responses after a pre-determined amount of time has passed. As you develop responses, there may also be new risks that must be identified, analyzed, and have responses planned.

The first step is to briefly review the risk for a thorough understanding of the provided analysis. Once the risk is well understood, identify at least one trigger. A risk trigger is an event, condition, or other sign that the risk is about to happen.

Next, identify a strategy for responding to the risk. As Section I previously indicated, the possible strategies for opportunities (positive risks) and threats (adverse risks) are:

Opportunity

Escalate: Make the organization aware of an opportunity outside of the initiative's scope or our authority, which may benefit the organization or the initiative. A higher level of the organization (e.g., portfolio, program, senior management) manages these risks.

Adopt: Take steps to ensure the realization of the benefits of the opportunity.

Enable: Increase the likelihood or impact of the opportunity.

Share: Share some of the benefits with a third party (e.g., form a partnership) to assure the realization of benefits.

Accept: Take advantage of the opportunity should it present itself, but do not actively pursue it.

Threat

Escalate: Make the organization aware of a threat outside of the initiative's scope or our authority, impacting the organization or initiative. A higher level of the organization (e.g., portfolio, program, senior management) manages these risks.

Avoid: Eliminate the threat such that the risk can no longer become an issue.

Accept: Acknowledge the threat will become an issue and take little or no further action. Damage control may be necessary if the threat becomes an issue.

Transfer: Shift the impact of the threat to a third party (e.g., purchase an insurance policy).

Mitigate: Reduce the likelihood or impact of the threat.

Tip: For agile projects, many risks, including those with strategies adopt, enable, avoid, or mitigate, may be added directly to the product backlog as added epics or stories.

Align the strategy with the priority of the risk. For example, do not accept a high priority risk or avoid one with low priority. See the next segment, *Aligning Response Strategies with Risk Priorities*, for more information. Develop a contingency plan describing the actions to take when the risk trigger is imminent or the risk has become a benefit or issue. In general, this plan must be:

- Cost and time effective when compared to the impact costs and time
- Aligned with the priority of the risk, the risk profile, and the initiative objectives
- SMART – Specific, Measurable, Achievable, Realistic, Timely
- Bought into by critical stakeholders

Fallback plans needed if the contingency plan is not sufficient may also be defined.

The process of defining contingency and fallback plans may identify additional risks by their actions. In this case, it is necessary to follow the risk assessment process and first categorize, define, analyze, and plan responses for these risks and document them in the risk log.

Review the defined response plan for potential impacts to initiative baseline plans (e.g., budgets and schedules). If necessary, formulate and document change requests to ensure response plans are followed. Change requests are essential for larger initiatives where separate teams manage the risk assessment process and define the risk responses.

Figure 24 illustrates the process graphically:

Figure 24: Risk Response Planning Process

To summarize the process:

1. Start with the highest priority risk - review the identification and analysis of the risk.
2. Identify at least one risk trigger. In the process, you may uncover additional information.
3. Select a response strategy aligned with the risk. For example, do not accept a high priority risk or avoid one with low priority.
4. Given the response strategy, plan and analyze response actions. Align them with the strategy, the organization's risk profile, and your initiative's objectives — document response actions in the risk log.
5. For the "avoid" and "adopt" strategies and any other responses with impacts on initiative plans, document with change requests as appropriate to ensure attainment of responses.

As part of response planning, new risks created by the responses may appear – be sure to route them through your overall risk management process.

Aligning Response Strategies with Risk Priorities

When determining the strategies and actions for risk response planning, it is best to start in the upper right-hand side of the risk assessment matrix for both opportunities and threats. Following this pattern ensures the handling of the highest priority risks first. While there may be some exceptions, the position and priority of risks in the matrix should also guide the response strategies:

- Include certain risk in all plans as an assumption (with a response strategy, typically adopt, enable, avoid, or mitigate)
- Adopt/avoid any risk with very high impact
- Passively accept any risk that is highly unlikely or very negligible in impact

The center of the matrix is split between share/enable (opportunities) and transfer/mitigate (threats). In general, those opportunities with a higher priority may require corrective actions to increase their likelihood and impact. In contrast, threats may require a decrease in probability or impact. Those risks with these responses are generally more difficult to purchase insurance for or partner with others, so transfer/share works typically better for center-left.

Figure 25 illustrates these potential actions graphically. Do not think of the boundaries as hard lines – risks on a border may need more careful consideration as to strategy.

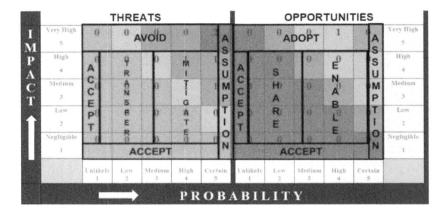

Figure 25: Risk Assessment Matrix Overlaid with Response Strategies

Figure 26 illustrates another graphical way of looking at the selection of response strategies based on increasing business value (amount at risk) and increasing severity (probability x impact). Note that while there are no black and white dividing lines in both cases, alignment is essential.

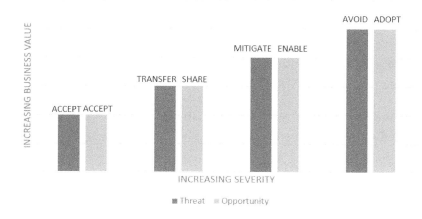

RISK RESPONSE STRATEGIES

Figure 26: Risk Response Strategies Based on Busines Value and Severity

Improving Decision Making Involving Uncertainty

The entire risk management process, including the risk assessment workshop and risk response planning, involves a great deal of decision-making. The best decisions are thoughtful and deliberate, consider all the relevant and available facts and information, and generally lead to better outcomes. One of the best ways to make a better decision is to follow the decision-making process.

Many decision-making frameworks and processes are available; however, a practical, fundamental method includes:

Define Decision Objectives: State the need for a decision along with any expectations, assumptions, and constraints that are known.

List Alternatives: Using brainstorming or other facilitated techniques, create a list of approximately three to five of the best alternatives that will meet the objectives. Deciding not to decide or "no decision" may be an acceptable alternative. For example, when accepting a risk, a contingency or fallback plan may not be necessary.

Analyze Alternatives: For each alternative, consider factors such as implementation time and costs, difficulty, risks, and whether the option is ethical.

Implement: Make a choice based on the analyzed information and proceed to implement the selected alternative.

Review Progress: If the implementation is not possible or proves to be more difficult than expected, other alternatives may be necessary. In the event of total failure, it may be required to re-review the objectives (e.g., were they reasonably defined, did we learn something in the process)

Figure 26 illustrates the process graphically:

Figure 27: A Basic Decision-Making Process

While the process is straightforward, take care to guard the process against cognitive bias. Cognitive bias is our natural tendency to view reality through our perceptions, filters, and experiences.

Cognitive psychology has defined more than a hundred types of biases, which may impact good decision-making (Buss 2005, Wikipedia 2020). Biases may occur from our perceptions of the objectives, alternatives, and even the presentation of the analysis's information.

Common cognitive biases that impact risk management include:

- **Positive thinking bias**: the tendency to be overly optimistic and give more weight to positive experiences
- **Negativity bias**: the tendency to give more weight to negative experiences
- **Framing effect**: drawing different conclusions from the same information, depending on the presentation of information
- **Confirmation bias**: the tendency to interpret information in a way that supports one's preconceptions
- **Prospect Theory**: a theory that decisions are made on gains and losses rather than on potential outcomes

Prospect Theory can play a significant role in allowing bias because we typically exaggerate small probabilities. This tendency creates "patterns" of risk attitudes that emerge and impact our thinking about risks:

- Risk-averse behavior when gains have moderate probabilities or losses have small probabilities
- Risk seeking behavior when losses have moderate probabilities or gains have small chances (Behavioral Economics 2021)

In general, there is no "cure" for cognitive bias. The best ways to minimize the risks of cognitive bias include:

- **Recognition** – become familiar with the types of biases
- **Strong facilitation** – make sure everyone has an equal voice in discussions
- **Follow processes** – doing things deliberately and thoughtfully will aid recognition and mitigation of bias
- **Change focus** – use of Six Thinking Hats is a perfect way to look at problems and solutions from all angles

Use of Contracts, Agreements, and Insurance

Contracts, other agreements, and various insurance types may help navigate uncertainty, especially threats uncovered during planning. Contracts and agreements tend to define the boundaries of uncertainty involved and responsible parties for bearing their impact. The three most common contract types are:

Contract Type	Advantages	Disadvantages
Fixed Price	<ul><li>Lowest buyer price risk</li><li>Seller motivated to control costs</li></ul>	<ul><li>Missing scope detail increases seller risk</li><li>Seller may not complete work if losing money</li><li>Seller may underbid to profit from change</li></ul>
Cost Reimbursable	<ul><li>Lower cost than fixed price since the seller does not need to manage risk as closely</li></ul>	<ul><li>Price risk since overall price unknown</li><li>Requires audits and effort to manage</li></ul>

		• Moderate incentive to control time and costs
Time & Materials	• Quick to create • Good for staff augmentation • Lowest seller risk	• Maximum buyer risk to price and time • Requires most buyer oversight • Highest buyer price risk

Table 3: Contract Types with Advantages and Disadvantages

Tip: Any of these contract types may include a financial incentive component, such as a bonus for meeting milestones or prices, to motivate the seller and reduce price or time risk for the buyer.

Insurers can cover nearly any risk, but the policies can be costly. Be sure there is a benefit for the initiative in taking this route. Some of the types of insurance available for initiatives include:

- Professional Liability (aka Errors and Omissions) covers the initiative and its manager and organization for mistakes and negligence. These are generally customized.
- Property to cover business assets. Usually does not protect from mass-destruction from flood or earthquake, which may require additional payments.
- Workers Compensation to cover injury or death of employees
- Product Liability to cover potential damages caused by products sold
- Business Interruption to cover disasters that cause a stoppage of work
- Inland Marine to cover land transportation of products, equipment, and other resources (Marine to cover sea transport)

Other forms of insurance may protect initiative team members who the organization legally employs – the human resources and payroll departments are the best sources of advice.

Re-computing Priorities, Finalize Cost and Time Budgets

It is "good enough" to prioritize the risks once during the workshop for many initiatives and maintain the priority. For those initiatives with many risks, it might be advantageous to re-prioritize them after planning risk response to reflect the result of a change by response actions. The re-prioritization will also require that EMV and ETV be re-computed to make them as accurate as possible. Those risks to consider for another look at prioritization are:

- Adopted opportunities
- Avoided threats
- Enabled opportunities
- Mitigated threats

Priorities will usually not change, even when reviewed for accuracy.

Review the EMV and the ETV values after response planning and re-prioritization—use of formulas rather than fixed numbers in the RAID log assists with automatic update.

With opportunity values negative (e.g., requiring less time and budget) and threat values positive, adding up the EMV and ETV columns provides a reasonable estimate for contingency reserves for adding to both budgets and schedules. Suppose your organization would instead use a fixed percentage. In that case, this is an opportunity to compare to the RAID log results and determine if there may be future issues.

Chapter Summary

Risk response planning tools and techniques include:

- A process for risk response planning
- Aligning response strategies with risk priorities
- Improving decision-making involving uncertainty
- Contracts, agreements, and insurance
- Re-computing priorities, finalizing cost and time reserves

CHAPTER 18

RISK MONITORING AND RESPONSE IMPLEMENTATION TOOLS AND TECHNIQUES

Key Risk Indicators

Data drives the best business decisions and risk monitoring. As risk monitoring begins, think about measures to collect and analyze to inform decisions. Where possible, data should inform the team of pending risk triggers. Smaller, less complicated projects can start with simple measures and spreadsheets. Larger enterprises may have more sophisticated identification and collection techniques.

Just as Key Performance Indicators (KPIs) are used to inform business decisions, key risk indicators (KRIs) are metrics to provide early warnings of risks. Examples of KRIs include:

- Collection of weather data to inform construction-work plans
- Collection of data about account payments to determine potential issues or benefits in accounts receivable

- Monitoring gasoline prices to determine business impacts (e.g., reduced travel spending or a shift from car travel to public transportation)
- Collecting data about the economy to predict consumer debt defaults

Tip: While some risk triggers may be black and white, on or off, many would benefit from the collection and analysis of appropriate data. If KRIs are essential to an initiative, consider reading *Developing Key Risk Indicators to Strengthen Enterprise Risk Management* (Beasley, Branson, and Hancock 2010).

Dealing with the Unknown - Worst Case Scenarios and Black Swans

Just as testing cannot prove the absence of defects, the most diligent risk assessment workshop will never identify all the risks. No matter how well planned and conducted, there is always something waiting, good or bad, to happen to initiatives. The waiting risks make it essential to focus on the most likely and most impactful events.

The most important actions are to plan for navigating uncertainty and conducting the best possible, most effective risk assessment workshop. Do not pretend bad things will not happen! Designing and conducting the workshop means the stakeholders and initiative team are better prepared to spot risk triggers and handle unidentified situations when they arise. It is very likely a mitigation strategy appropriate for the unknown event was a part of a prior discussion.

Another form of worst-case scenario has become known as a "black swan". These are surprise events that have a devastating impact. In hindsight, they are inappropriately categorized as something we should have predicted and been able to handle (Taleb 2010). One of my early projects experienced a black swan.

Before risk management was a part of the PMBOK, I worked as a technical resource for a company that did not manage risk particularly well. Bad decisions impacted a significant project. But then the unthinkable happened. The FBI arrested the Chief Programmer of a new operating system for tax evasion. Management denied this was going to impact the project. They rationalized that he would return to work while on bail and awaiting trial.

But to make matters worse, once out on bail, he fled the country. Unfortunately, no one knew as much about the system as this team member, so no one could step in and save the project. And management inaction cost nearly a month to pass.

Now I would not expect any risk assessment workshop to identify these specific circumstances. However, I would hope that if there were crucial and irreplaceable resources involved, these risks would be identified and addressed. For human resources, this might mean having a transition and succession plan. Or at least making sure the division of work supported success. And most of all, taking some form of immediate yet well-thought-out corrective action once the event occurred. Not only did the project end in failure, but this event triggered the downward slide of the entire company.

If necessary, the planner should, without the team, give some consideration to the worst-case scenarios. These are the types of things we see in everyday news, such as:

- A hack of a financial institution that jeopardized the personal data of millions
- A workplace mass shooting that disrupts work and removes essential resources
- A fire causing $2B of damage and requiring years of reconstruction
- A nuclear disaster and tsunami impacting events in a city more than 100 miles away

Keep in mind that these events need not happen directly to an initiative. A disaster in a city may require additional security to make attendees comfortable at an event occurring a day later. Identify and consult a list of potential scenarios when making financial and other major initiative decisions. Following the robust process developed around the risk assessment framework can help embrace significant benefits and ward off catastrophic events.

When Threats Turn into a Crisis

Establishing good communications, public relations, and using our soft skills as we move forward is a good strategy for preparing for a crisis. Risk communications need to address the issues of surprise events and loss of control. Think about product recalls. By quickly admitting fault and recalling products, companies limit the damages to both their financials and their reputation.

Perhaps the most famous case illustrating these points is the Chicago Tylenol murders in 1982. Johnson & Johnson's actions to reduce deaths and warn the public of poisoning risks have been widely praised as an excellent public relations response to such a crisis. They immediately issued advisories to pharmacies and hospitals, halted Tylenol production, and quickly conducted a nationwide recall of over 31 million bottles (Emsley 2008). These types of actions help build consumer trust.

After the event and initial actions, the stakeholders' reactions need to be carefully observed for additional signs of how to mitigate issues and rebuild trust. These observations led to reforms in both drug packaging and federal anti-tampering laws.

Trust is essential, especially for fixed constraint initiatives. Teams with high levels of trust can operate more efficiently and work better together to reach common goals. Trust can also be built by understanding stakeholders' motivations and addressing their needs through communications and engaging activities. One activity may be to engage the initiative sponsor and senior management in making the acceptance plan. The acceptance plan outlines what the initiative will achieve and how they will know it has been completed.

Many more extensive and more complex initiatives can benefit from a public relations program carefully designed to focus on initiative value. Such campaigns can be used to mitigate risks, gain general acceptance, and maintain project transparency. Let us look at some of the qualities to include in your public relations program:

- *Anticipate information requirements* to address potential issues or concerns proactively, or at least have key answers at your fingertips. The key ingredient is quality information, which stresses the benefits of the project without focusing on issues. An essential step to achieving this is to be certain risk communications are included in the risk register or RAID log.
- *Deliver information in formats and using facilities friendly to stakeholders.* Showing genuine care and concern for

stakeholders and their needs and expressing genuine interest in their inquiries goes a long way in building trust and ensuring receipt of critical messages. This includes communicating in clear and concise language, which will inform all stakeholders.

- *Invite stakeholders to participate in decisions* that will enhance the value of the initiative for them.
- *Empower the team to solve urgent problems* since the manager cannot be everywhere and observing all situations.
- *Anticipate information requirements to make sure responses are timely.* You also want to be sure they are flexible and do not paint you into a corner. For example, a division of a well-known corporation announced a "first annual" event without a solid plan to deliver annually. They looked foolish the following year when budget constraints meant they could not repeat the event.
- *Make sure that responses to any threats are quick, impressive, and communicated to the necessary stakeholders.*

Preparing for the Future

Preparing for the future should begin with the first risk management plan and risk assessment workshop. At the end of each step of the process, the initiative manager should stop, reflect on the step, and prepare to enhance the effort in the future. The risk management plan developed should generally replace the template for the next initiative. In general, this requires no more than 30-60 minutes, so please do not bypass this step.

When the risk assessment workshop nears completion, one of the final sessions should spend time (usually 30 minutes or less) to gauge team attitudes toward the process and collect lessons.

As initiatives move forward, take some steps to continue to identify and support future improvements:

- Record the small wins – benefits of identified opportunities and avoided impacts of threats.
- Speak with the team and key stakeholders frequently to get their thoughts.
- Review all high-priority risks with project sponsors and other key stakeholders. Ask for their sign-off on proposed actions.
- Take notes about observations as work goes forward – start a lessons-learned list for the process.
- At the end of the initiative, conduct a lessons-learned and dedicate some time to discuss the process of navigating uncertainty.
- For the next initiative, translate the lessons into actions by choosing a small number of improvements.

Preparation for the next initiative and workshop should include starting a checklist of risks and planning for continuous improvement. Once the risk log achieves closure, review the list of identified risks, and consider which might apply to other organization initiatives. Starting a checklist means these risks will be a part of the next risk assessment workshop, leaving the team to focus on new or more significant risks.

Continuous improvement is about making ongoing improvements to future initiatives. The most widely used tool for continuous improvement is the four-step model, also known as the Deming or Shewhart Cycle. The four-step model checks the efficiency of a change on a small scale before full-scale implementation. Base decisions to move to full-scale implementation on data. The four-step model, also referred to as Plan-Do-Check-Act (PDCA), is based on the scientific method: hypothesis – experiment – evaluation (ASQ 2021).

As previously mentioned in this book, a few small changes I have identified over the years that are important to consider while moving forward and improving the risk management method:

- Connect any risk response actions with business strategies and priorities; align the responses with the risk response strategies.
- Consider if there should be some goals to identify several opportunities – these are typically harder to identify, and it is common to associate risk management with threats.
- Consider how to avoid group-think and cognitive biases from risk assessment workshops.

Now is the time to review all the lessons-learned and attitudes recorded and draw up a short plan for identifying and testing improvements for future iterations.

Chapter Summary

Risk monitoring and response implementation tools and techniques include:

- Key risk indicators (KRI)
- Worst-case scenarios
- Knowing how to handle threats that escalated into crises
- Preparing for the future

REFERENCES

ASQ. "PDCA Cycle - What Is the Plan-Do-Check-Act Cycle? | ASQ." ASQ. Accessed February 13, 2021. https://asq.org/quality-resources/pdca-cycle.

———. "What Is a Fishbone Diagram? Ishikawa Cause & Effect Diagram | ASQ." ASQ. Accessed February 13, 2021. https://asq.org/quality-resources/fishbone.

Beasley, M., B. Branson, and B. Hancock. "Developing Key Risk Indicators to Strengthen Enterprise Risk Management." COSO, 2010. Accessed November 1, 2017. https://www.coso.org/Documents/COSO-KRI-Paper-Full-FINAL-for-Web-Posting-Dec110-000.pdf.

BehavioralEconomics. "Prospect Theory." BehavioralEconomics.com | The BE Hub. Accessed February 13, 2021. https://www.behavioraleconomics.com/resources/mini-encyclopedia-of-be/prospect-theory/.

Buss, David M., ed. The Handbook of Evolutionary Psychology. Hoboken, NJ: John Wiley & Sons, 2005.

Champlain College. "Appreciative Inquiry Commons." The Appreciative Inquiry Commons. Accessed November 1, 2017. https://appreciativeinquiry.champlain.edu/.

Cook, John D. "The Titanic Effect." John D. Cook Consulting (blog), October 18, 2010. https://www.johndcook.com/blog/2010/10/18/titanic-effect/.

De Bono, Edward. Six Thinking Hats. Rev. and Updated ed. London: Penguin Books, 2000.

Emsley, John. Molecules of Murder: Criminal Molecules and Classic Cases. Cambridge, UK: RSC Pub, 2008.

Gomer, Justin, and Jackson Hille. "An Essential Guide to SWOT Analysis." Columbia University, July 14, 2015. http://mci.ei.columbia.edu/files/2012/12/An-Essential-Guide-to-SWOT-Analysis.pdf.

Hall, D.C., and D.T Hulett. "Universal Risk Project - Final Report," February 2002. https://02f0a56ef46d93f03c90-

22ac5f107621879d5667e0d7ed595bdb.ssl.cf2.rackcdn.com/sites
/785/uploads/7224/Universal_RIsk_Project_Final_Report_Feb_2
00220151002-4513-tsh2gk.pdf.

IAF. "IAF World | IAF World." Accessed November 1, 2017.
https://www.iaf-world.org/site/index.php.

ISO. "Risk Management: ISO31000." International Organization for
Standardization. Accessed August 18, 2019.
https://www.iso.org/files/live/sites/isoorg/files/store/en/PUB10
0426.pdf.

Johannessen, K.B., G. Oettingen, and D. Mayer. "Mental Contrasting
of a Dieting Wish Improves Self-Reported Health Behaviour."
Psychology & Health 27, no. sup2 (October 2012): 43–58.
https://doi.org/10.1080/08870446.2011.626038.

Kletter, David. "Booz Allen Hamilton." Institute for Operations
Research and Management Science (INFORMS), August 18, 2019.
https://www.informs.org/Impact/O.R.-Analytics-Success-
Stories/Industry-Profiles/Booz-Allen-Hamilton.

Lim, Rosanne. "Top 10 Main Causes of Project Failure." Project
Management Articles (blog), June 4, 2019. https://project-
management.com/top-10-main-causes-of-project-failure/.

Marr, Bernard. "Why Successful People Love Bad News," February
10, 2014. https://www.linkedin.com/pulse/20140210102648-
64875646-why-successful-people-love-bad-news.

McCaffrey, Tony. Brainswarming: Because Brainstorming Doesn't
Work, 2014.
https://hbr.org/video/3373616535001/brainswarming-because-
brainstorming-doesnt-work.

Meredith, Jack R, Scott M Shafer, Samuel J Mantel, and Margaret
Sutton. Project Management in Practice. Danvers, Mass: Wiley,
2014.

Mikitani, Mickey. "Discovering Frameworks," October 15, 2013.
https://www.linkedin.com/pulse/20131015115306-52782505-
discovering-frameworks.

———. "Shikumi: The Power of Frameworks." Rakuten Today,
August 30, 2019. https://rakuten.today/mickeysvoice/shikumi-
power-frameworks.html.

MindTools. "Cause and Effect Analysis: Identifying the Likely Causes of Problems." MindTools. Accessed November 1, 2017. http://www.mindtools.com/pages/article/newTMC_03.htm.

———. "Force Field Analysis: Analyzing the Pressures For and Against Change." MindTools. Accessed November 1, 2017. http://www.mindtools.com/pages/article/newTED_06.htm.

PMI, ed. A Guide to the Project Management Body of Knowledge (PMBOK Guide). Fifth edition. Newtown Square, Pennsylvania: Project Management Institute, Inc, 2013.

———. "Capturing the Value of Project Management." Pulse of the Profession. PMI, February 2015. https://www.pmi.org/learning/thought-leadership/pulse/capturing-the-value-of-project-management.

———. "The High Cost of Low Performance." Pulse of the Profession. PMI, March 2013. https://www.pmi.org/learning/thought-leadership/pulse/the-high-cost-of-low-performance-2013.

RAND. "Delphi Method." RAND Corporation. Accessed August 18, 2019. https://www.rand.org/topics/delphi-method.html.

Scheid, Jean. "Examples of Poor Risk Management Causing a Project to Fail." Bright Hub PM (blog), November 10, 2009. https://www.brighthubpm.com/risk-management/55492-examples-of-poor-risk-management-causing-a-project-to-fail/.

Standish Group. "The CHAOS Report," 1995. https://www.projectsmart.co.uk/white-papers/chaos-report.pdf.

Tague, Nancy R. The Quality Toolbox. 2nd ed. Milwaukee, Wis: ASQ Quality Press, 2005.

Taleb, Nassim Nicholas. The Black Swan: The Impact of the Highly Improbable. New York: Random House, 2010.

Vargas, R. "Adopting the Quadratic Mean Process to Quantify the Qualitative Risk Analysis." SlideShare, October 27, 2013. https://www.slideshare.net/ricardo.vargas/2013-10-27ricardovargasquadraticmeanenpmiweb.

Wikipedia. "Business Model." In Wikipedia, February 5, 2021. https://en.wikipedia.org/w/index.php?title=Business_model&oldid=1005049567.

———. "Cognitive Bias Mitigation." In Wikipedia, December 6, 2020. https://en.wikipedia.org/w/index.php?title=Cognitive_bias_miti gation&oldid=992585753.

———. "Transportation Safety in the United States." In Wikipedia, February 9, 2021. https://en.wikipedia.org/w/index.php?title=Transportation_safe ty_in_the_United_States&oldid=1005830814.

Yazdanifard, Rashad, and Kaizer Boikanyo Ratsiepe. "Poor Risk Management as One of the Major Reasons Causing Failure of Project Management." In Proceedings of the 2011 International Conference on Management and Service Science. Wuhan China, 2011.Beasley, M., B. Branson, and B. Hancock. 2010. *Developing Key Risk Indicators to Strengthen Enterprise Risk Management.* COSO. December. Retrieved from https://www.coso.org/Documents/COSO-KRI-Paper-Full-FINAL-for-Web-Posting-Dec110-000.pdf.

APPENDIX

APPENDIX A: RAID RISK TAB COLUMNS

Column	Column Header	Description	Notes
A	No.	Identification/ reference number	Automatically populated when Add New Risk Button pressed
B	Date Last Updated	Date this risk was last modified	
C	Date Raised	Date this risk was raised	Automatically populated when Add New Risk Button pressed
D	Raised By	Initials/name of person or group raising the risk	
E	Category	Risk category from sources of risk	Possible dropdown[3] values: Client Driven Externally Driven Internally Driven Regulatory Driven PLC Driven

---

[3] All drop-down values can be found on the (Lookup) tab

			Unknown Unknowns; value is provided to dashboard
F	Opportunity or Threat Description	Complete description of the opportunity or threat	
G	Potential Benefits/ Exposures	Description of the benefits of the opportunity or impacts of threats	Include specific dollar and time amounts of the impacts when reasonably known (e.g., a $1,000 exposure, a 10-day benefit to the schedule). These will be looked at in more detail when computed EMV and ETV, columns Q and R.
H	Probability	Probability of risk	Possible dropdown values: 1-Unlikely 2-Low 3-Medium 4-High 5-Certain; value is provided to dashboard
I	Impact	Impact of risk	Possible dropdown values: 1-Negligible 2-Low 3-Medium 4-High 5-Very High; value is provided to dashboard
J-L	Reserved	Reserved for future use	Keep these columns collapsed
M	Severity	Risk priority	Automatically calculated as Probability x Impact
N	Dashboard Flag Column	Used by Dashboard only	Automatically populated when Probability, Impact, and Strategy are chosen; keep column collapsed
O	Status	Status of risk	Possible dropdown values:

			Closed Duplicate Further Investigation Identified Realized (is issue/benefit) Rejected; value is provided to dashboard
P	Strategy	Risk response strategy aligned to severity	Possible dropdown values: Avoid (Threat) Accept (Threat) Transfer (Threat) Mitigate (Threat) Escalate (Threat) Adopt (Opportunity) Enable (Opportunity) Share (Opportunity) Accept (Opportunity) Escalate (Opportunity); value is provided to dashboard
Q	EMV	Estimated monetary value	Negative for opportunity, positive for threat
R	ETV	Estimated time value	Negative for opportunity, positive for threat
S	Mitigation/ Contingency Plan/ Actions/ Results	Descriptions of all agreed-upon actions to be taken	
T	Risk Manager	Person responsible for enacting the response when trigger imminent	
U	Response Cost	Cost of implementing the actions	**Be sure to update EMV when this is known
V	Response Time	Time for implementing the actions	**Be sure to update ETV when this is known
W	Date Finalized	Date the risk is closed	

Table 4: RAID Tab Risk Column Definitions

APPENDIX B

Appendix B: License to Use and Modify Templates and Instructional Materials

Book buyers are granted access to a set of tools and templates, which are provided "as is" and may be freely used and modified to meet their needs. Of course, we always appreciate the recognition as the source of the templates. And for those who might need additional help, we offer both training and consulting. Materials from our other publications (e.g., Accidental Project Manager: Zero to Hero in 7 Days) are accessible in the same location. Please visit https://accidentalpm.online/downloads to access these materials. After registration, a process that takes thirty seconds or less, an account will be established, a link and password emailed to you, and the downloads will be accessible in your library.

For instructors who use this book for their classes, additional materials are available, including PowerPoint slide decks of lectures based on this book and experiential, project-based exercises for students. Once again, please feel free to modify to suit initiatives. As always, we appreciate at least a slide or a few sentences acknowledging the materials' source. Please visit https://accidentalpm.online/instructor to access these materials. After registration, a process that takes thirty seconds or less, an account will be established, a link and password emailed to you, and the downloads will be accessible in your library. To maintain access, please provide us with proof of the class and the text within 48 hours. Proof could be through a course or training catalog description, book order receipt, or other appropriate evidence.

In the rare event that you do not receive an email with your account information, you can sign on at https://accidentalpm.online/login, use your email address, and click the "Forgot Password" link.

Need assistance with our site or meeting the specified conditions? Please contact us at support@ppcgroup.us.

Index

Accidental Project Manager:
The Online Experience

PLAN TO MANAGE PROJECTS SUCCESSFULLY!

- Learn the fundamental concepts and terms
- Take the training anywhere, anytime, on any device
- Earn a Project Hero social badge from Accredible

If you are an aspiring, new, or accidental project manager, this course, which goes beyond the book, is for you. Your instructor has over 20 years of project management experience and has three Amazon international best-selling books on project management.

Upon completing the course and spending at least 23 hours engaged with it, you will earn your Project Hero social badge from Accredible. You also meet your training requirement for the CAPM® certification.

While you may complete the course in as few as seven days, you will have access for six months. During this time, you will have access to any changes, updates, upgrades, and new materials added during that time. You keep all downloaded materials.

As a valued reader, you can join our Project Hero Academy free and enjoy a $100 discount on the course. Visit https://www.accidentalpm.online/project-hero-academy to see if you qualify.

BE SURE TO GET YOUR FREE TEMPLATES!

As a valued reader, you have access to all the templates referenced in this book and those that accompany our other books!

Sign up for access (you keep the downloads, plus they are in your online library) at:

accidentalpm.online/downloads

Bonus: Our PM Best Practices and Tips will be delivered once a month to your inbox.

Made in the USA
Las Vegas, NV
25 November 2022

60294722R00125